DEATH CARRIES A CAMCORDER

Books by Tom Simon

Lord Talon's Revenge
The Worm of the Ages and Other Tails
Writing Down the Dragon and Other Essays
Style is the Rocket and Other Essays on Writing

THE EYE OF THE MAKER
The End of Earth and Sky
The Grey Death (forthcoming)

Visit the author's website at
bondwine.com

DEATH CARRIES
A CAMCORDER
and Other Essays

BY

TOM SIMON

Calgary
BONDWINE BOOKS
2014

Edited by Robin Eytchison
Cover design by Sarah Huntrods

Published by Bondwine Books
First paperback edition, June 2016
ISBN 978-0-9881292-7-6

TABLE OF CONTENTS

PREFACE

For in Calormen, story-telling (whether the stories are true or made up) is a thing you're taught, just as English boys and girls are taught essay-writing. The difference is that people want to hear the stories, whereas I never heard of anyone who wanted to read the essays.

—C. S. Lewis, *The Horse and His Boy*

Montaigne used the French word *essai*, meaning 'attempt' or 'experiment', as a name for the short, often breezy pieces he wrote to express his personal thoughts and opinions. Somehow the English word *essay* has lost about half of that original meaning. For countless people, I am afraid, an essay is just a bit of writing ground out joylessly to make an artificial argument, usually at the orders of somebody's English teacher. It is written without love or interest, and as Lewis said, nobody wants to read it.

The pieces in this book, I hope, are not much like that. They are set down here almost exactly as I wrote them. I like to think of them as *essais* in Montaigne's sense, rather than essays in the dull modern sense, and I use the French word, not because I am terribly pretentious, but to remind myself (and my readers) not to take them too seriously. I am not Moses carving the Ten Commandments on stone; I am not even a student grinding his way through a degree in English Literature. I am only a writer of far-fetched stories; and like most writers, I find that the easiest way to discover what I think is to try and write it down.

In Lewis's terms, I would rather not think of these as essays, but as a special kind of story: the story of an idea as it made its way round in my head, bumping into other ideas and sometimes striking sparks off them. I hope they may strike more sparks as they continue their journey with you.

At the time of this writing, all these *essais* (and a good many others) can be found at my website. I am collecting them in a book in the hope that they may reach a slightly wider audience, and also because some of my readers have expressed a desire to have them in a more permanent and convenient form.

TOM SIMON
Calgary
September 2014

DEATH CARRIES A CAMCORDER

Fiction is, among many other things, a game between writer and reader, a kind of mental strip-tease in which the writer slowly reveals the details of the story, and the reader tries to guess at their significance. Mystery stories exhibit the game in its purest form, of course; but the element of guessing 'whodunit' turns up in every kind of fiction.

As stories have grown more complex, and the telling more elliptical and compressed, guessing out the storyteller's meaning has become a difficult and demanding skill. Usually we don't think of it in those terms, because *as readers*, we began to develop that skill early in childhood; it was fun to do, and after all, children can take delight in the most fiendishly elaborate games. Generally speaking, we don't notice the skill involved until it stops working – that is, until the writer breaks the rules of the game. Then our involvement in the story goes up in a puff of what is sometimes known as 'fridge logic'. All the inconsistencies, the factual errors, the implausible connections and narrative slip-ups, which we ignored as long as we were *inside* the story, come back to us in a rush, and we can never enter imaginatively into that story again.

To prevent this, writers have developed a complex vocabulary of cues and signals, to let the reader know when she is receiving the straight goods and when the writer (or a character) is deliberately misleading her.

9

The largest part of this technique falls under the heading of point of view. This simplifies the game and reduces most of it to one question: *Who is the narrator, and what does he know?*

A first-person narrator is expected to be generally truthful, unless he 'accidentally' betrays, early in the story, that he is a liar and his words need to be sifted. Even if he is lying, we expect the lies to be self-serving – attempts to colour and distort facts that we might find out from some other source, rather than to invent a narrative from whole cloth unrelated to the truth. If the narrator is making up a story that is fictitious *within the context of another made-up story,* and that framing story is not even told, the reader is going to laugh bitterly at the whole pointless exercise and put down the book. Not even Borges cared to risk *that* kind of recursive knot.

If the story is written in 'close third', so that we follow one character's thoughts and perceptions at a time, we know that the narrative is subject to the limitations and biases of that character's knowledge; but we also have a corrective, for we trust the omniscient author's *selection* of the viewpoint character. The writer may not, at any given moment, have chosen the character who gives us the most truthful or accurate account of the facts; but we have faith that all the essential facts will be there in the end, and discoverable, so that we will get all the elements we need to make sense of the story.

The extreme points of view, which are also the simplest, are always assumed to be reliable, because they allow us no other imaginative angle from which to correct their unreliability. If the story is told in a camera-eye viewpoint, we expect the camera to function properly and to record faithfully everything that it sees. If the story is told by an omniscient narrator, we expect the narrator to remain true to the facts he has already laid down. In Chapter One of an omniscient tale, anything goes; but Chapter Two is limited, for the things already said in Chapter One are as the law of the Medes and the Persians, which altereth not. And if Chapter Twenty-five sees the author painted into a corner, so that *no* consistent interpretation of events is possible, then we expect him to go back to Chapter Four and cleverly put a door in that part of the room *before* releasing his work to the public.

These are the general laws of the game – we may call them the laws of narrative protocol –which we as writers break at our peril. But there are other laws, the laws of character and conflict, which sometimes clash with them; it is our job to make sure that the clash never occurs – and if it does, we must edit it out. Repainting will not do; we must go back and put in that extra door in Chapter Four, or make still larger alterations to the structure, until the rules of viewpoint and the nature of the story run smoothly together. Everything that exists for a reason *outside* the story (to convey information to the reader) must also have a reason *inside* the story; at the very least, there should be no reason inside the story why it should not happen.

In particular, we have to make sure that the story is being told by someone who could plausibly tell it. Someone identified only as 'rysmiel' left this comment when Sherwood Smith discussed the question:

> I have a strong dislike for first-person narratives where there is no inherent reason for the narrator to be writing this stuff down, nor context in which they could reasonably have done so. I particularly don't like this when the narrative gives away terrible secrets, or casually mentions things that would be liable to send the writer/protagonist to jail. It's not a book-killer, but it will reliably make me fume. First person narratives should have a reason for existing, and unless they are explicitly diaries there should be an assumed person they are written *for*.

This is exactly the reaction we can expect our readers to have if we violate narrative protocol. When it happens, we have no excuse or defence: if we saw in the first draft that this problem was going to arise, we should have chosen a different protocol and rewritten as required. We should have put that door in Chapter Four.

In the drama, when an actor directly addresses the audience (in character, not in the polite exordium that used to be common in plays) or otherwise interacts with it, they call it 'breaking the fourth wall'. It is permissible as a form of comic relief, and in certain kinds of 'experimental' theatre, but in general it's a no-no, and has been ever since they discontinued the iniquitous practice of putting high-priced seats right on the stage. The novel is much more forgiving about the fourth wall, because the author is permitted, indeed expected, to make up his own rules about it. But once he has made the rules, we expect him to play fair and stick by them. If he doesn't, any but the least attentive reader is likely to find herself bounced right out of the story, 'looking at the little abortive Secondary World from outside', as Tolkien put it. Storytelling is very like a mild form of hypnotism, and if the hypnotist violates his subject's trust in any obvious or startling way, he will almost certainly break the trance.

At one time, when stories were recited and not read, it was usual to exalt the storyteller's vanity over the reader's intelligence, by including all kinds of dramatic 'turns' that would allow the *skald* or *scop* to show off his histrionic skills, at no matter what cost in narrative probability. The most famous 'turn' is, of course, the high-flown speech made by a heroic character on the point of death. If he is slain in battle, then the battle itself must stop to listen while he makes his declamation; nay more, even his blood must stop flowing, and if his lungs have been punctured by arrows, they must somehow do their office long enough to give the ham his moment in the limelight. It is the same impulse that forced composers and librettists to write beautiful dying-swan arias for their expiring divas.

Now, when a story is *recited*, that is, when it is treated as a dramatic performance, this kind of trumpery is permissible, if ill-advised. But when the story is written to be *read*, the matter is more difficult. Instead of putting our trust in the bard, we put it in an invisible narrator, a harder thing for most of us to do. We are always tempted to ask such questions as: 'Is this true?' 'Does this make sense?' And above all, 'But how do you *know*?' And the wilder and more improbable the story, the more careful the writer has to be to give, or at least solidly imply, plausible answers to these questions. It is dangerous to let the reader think too much about the narrative assumptions of the story, but it cannot always be prevented. It is fatal to let her reach the conclusion that you are not playing by your own rules.

I have written about one of the most annoying ways in which an author can violate his own protocols. In *Report on Probability A*, Brian Aldiss sets up an elaborate game with point of view, based on the rather precious idea that none of his characters are willing to make even the most obvious assumptions about each other's psychology – that they are all human, for instance, or that the articulate noises coming out of their mouths are in fact English words. But he is grossly inconsistent, for his characters are continually slipping and making assumptions about each other's thoughts and motives. Worse yet, they know things that they could not possibly have observed. One character thinks that his broken clock might still work, but is afraid to wind it up and prove himself wrong. We find this out from the supposedly objective, camera-eye report written by another character watching him from afar. The best camera in the world could never observe any such thing, and if it could, we would have no grounds at all for doubting one another's psychological makeup. Aldiss bursts the bubble of Secondary Belief, not once but with dreary and deliberate regularity, by this same elementary blunder. And since the game is the entire plot and point of the story, once the rules are broken, the remainder of the tale equals nothing.

You can buy entire how-to-write books that deal with nothing but point of view: first person, second person (rare and inadvisable), limited third, omniscient third, camera eye, deep penetration, and the fabled 'M' structure. The list reads like a *Kama Sutra* of voyeurism. Many readers are obsessively concerned with these details; getting them wrong is a quick and sure way to lose them.

It was not always so. The omniscient point of view was good enough for almost every writer of fiction until the advent of the novel in the 18th century. The degree of 'penetration' varied, of course. In *Beowulf*, I am reliably informed, there is only one line in which we are made privy to a character's interior mental processes: 'his breast boiled with dark thoughts, as was not his custom'. But we are not told any details about the dark thoughts, and Beowulf goes right on with his preparations to fight the dragon. As long as narratives were so little concerned with psychology, and so much with action, point of view was not important enough to take trouble about. The question is not even raised, for instance, in Aristotle's *Poetics*. In the Greek epic, it is taken for granted that the narrator knows the whole story and tells it reliably; in drama, of course, the question does not even arise.

Then Defoe gave us first-person narration, and Richardson followed up with the epistolary novel, the first form that really encouraged the exploration of multiple characters' thoughts. The psychological novel burst on the scene, and nobody since has been able to tell a story in quite the naive, old-fashioned way. We have to *worry* about these things now.

A century later, Edgar Allan Poe perfected the unreliable narrator, and so we must also question at every moment whether our storyteller is telling lies. We are playing a constant and intricate detective game with our texts, and this has become so integral to our reading of novels that we almost feel cheated if a narrator proves *too* reliable.

But in fantasy, and to a lesser extent in SF and other imaginative literatures, it is vital that the narrative be reliable and controlled. We must always be able to distinguish between impossible events in 'reality' (the characters' reality) and mere illusions or hallucinations, even if the characters themselves cannot. The default assumption must be that any event, however bizarre, is essentially what it appears to be; and if we violate that assumption without giving clear cues, our readers will be furious because we have violated their trust. I have made this error myself, and reaped the consequences in sufficient abundance.

Nobody knew this better than J. R. R. Tolkien, who expended enormous effort to give his fantasies a solid air of *vera historia*. The Appendices, prologues and footnotes, the maps and other impedimenta of *The Lord of the Rings*, all serve to build up a massive and unquestionable assurance of the fundamental consistency and honesty of the text. One could almost believe that there really was a Red Book of Westmarch, painstakingly translated by modern scholarship, and that one is getting a glimpse of the history and culture of a former world. Nobody else has taken the same degree of trouble, which is one reason why so much other fantasy seems arbitrary and frivolous by comparison.

It is amazing how consistently Tolkien accounts for everything said to be written in the Red Book. There are no windy death-speeches, no reports on events that did not come from a surviving eyewitness. We never meet Sauron, not because Tolkien wants to keep his Ultimate Evil vague and depersonalized (a frequent and foolish accusation), but simply because 'those who pass the gates of Barad-dûr do not return'. We are made privy to Gollum's thoughts only because of his habit of ceaselessly talking to himself, and we never glimpse the soul of an Orc. Indeed, when we come closest, in the talk between Shagrat and Gorbag at Cirith Ungol, Tolkien takes care to explain how Sam was able to understand Orkish (by the power of the Ring, of course, greatly increased by proximity to Mordor). In some of the outtakes from *The Return of the King,* he goes still further, specifying the periods after the Field of Cormallen when Frodo shut himself up in a room in Minas Tirith to write the copious notes that he brought back to Bilbo at Rivendell. And at the very end we see the Red Book itself, eighty chapters long, bringing the story down to Frodo's departure for the Grey Havens. I cannot think of anything so scrupulously buttressed in all of literature before it.

But even Tolkien nods. The most beautiful face may be marred by a tiny flaw that would pass unnoticed on a person of average looks, and the most meticulous argument can be spoilt by a venial error. Only once does Tolkien slip and tell us the thoughts of someone who could not possibly have been interviewed by the authors of the Red Book:

> A fox passing through the wood on business of his own stopped several minutes and sniffed.
> 'Hobbits!' he thought. 'Well, what next? I have heard of strange doings in this land, but I have seldom heard of a hobbit sleeping out of doors under a tree. Three of them! There's something mighty queer behind this.' He was quite right, but he never found out any more about it.

The temptation is strong to make excuses for this lapse. It could have been put there to signalize (for this is quite early in *Fellowship*, when the hobbits are still in the Shire) that this part of the Red Book was written by Bilbo, a less truthful and more florid narrator than Frodo. Other pleas could doubtless be devised. But in fact it is pure fiction, *even within the characters' own frame of reference,* because all three hobbits were fast asleep when this is supposed to have happened. Nobody ever saw the fox again, or asked him his opinion of the matter; nobody even had any way of knowing he had been there.

Really, this is nothing more than the last faint twitch of the twee, talking-down, children's-bedtime-story reflex that so damaged *The Hobbit* (in Tolkien's own opinion). There were considerably many such touches in the first drafts of 'the new Hobbit', but Tolkien rooted them out with great thoroughness and industry in the revision. Only this one remains, like a lone outcrop of rock in a level plain where once great mountains stood. I always stumble when I read this passage, and marvel that Tolkien let the book go to press in two successive editions without excising it.

It is this kind of thing that prevents me from taking *A Song of Ice and Fire* as seriously as Tolkien's work. Martin, like the *scops* of old, plays the ham with Death. Addicted to visceral thrills, he cannot resist the temptation to show us a character's dying thoughts and feelings, even when the character dies alone. I cannot now put my finger on a good example, for the books are very ill organized, but the body count is enormous and suitable examples should not be difficult to find. Every time he resorts to this device, I am reminded that I am only reading a novel, after all, and I am distanced from the characters and their plight. The extreme violence of the situations combines with the careless abuse of narrative integrity like a binary poison, so that far from intensifying my experience of the story, it vitiates the impact and leaves me regarding the text coldly and critically from outside.

This is not a fatal fault, but it is a grievous one. Like the tiny flaw in the otherwise perfect face, it is more disfiguring to a good book than to a bad one. Martin is a brilliant writer, but he falls just short of being a great one, partly because he continually undermines himself by these small bouts of self-indulgence. 'Show, don't tell,' like all rules, should not be followed off a cliff. Martin not only follows it off cliffs, he makes Death keep his camcorder running right to the moment when the body is smashed to jelly on the jagged rocks below.

ZENO'S MOUNTAINS

According to local legend, one of the first tourists to visit Calgary (then a Northwest Mounted Police fort with a few civilian outbuildings) was an Englishman of energetic habits but not, it seems, with any wide experience of the world. One morning, having rested from the rigours of his journey, he decided to take his morning constitutional by walking to the Rocky Mountains and back.

In those days you could see the mountains easily from the N.W.M.P. fort, small but sharp and clear on the western horizon. In England, of course, nothing looks sharp and clear more than a few miles away. In that mild and humid air, every distant object is more or less obscured and coloured by haze: minor English poets can always eke out their verses with facile rubbish about 'blue remembered hills'. In the dry cold highlands of Alberta, there is no such haze; objects on the horizon, on a sunny day, are very nearly as clear as those immediately at hand. But our English tourist knew nothing of this, and set out with the idea of visiting the mountains and getting back to the fort in time for breakfast.

Five or six miles out, the Englishman, who must already have been rather footsore and perplexed, clambered up the long ridge that would later be called Signal Hill. Cresting the ridge, he would have been appalled to discover a wide plain sloping gently *down* for several miles before him. Beyond that rose the first tumbled range of the true foothills, towards which, disappointed but not daunted, he plodded on. Behind that range is the Kananaskis valley, and then the last range of foothills before the beginning of the actual mountains – some fifty miles west of Fort Calgary as the crow flies.

Several days later, a searching party found the Englishman and brought him back to the fort to recuperate.

Something rather similar happens to writers who visit Elfland; even to-day, when the map of that country has been scribbled over with marked trails and motorways, the lesson of *distance* is one that every traveller must discover for himself. It is notoriously a place where journeys take longer than expected: short stories turn into novels, and novels turn into trilogies, and trilogies turn into the high felony that has sometimes been called 'Aggravated Trilogy' in the statute-books of the critics. This has been going on as long as people have been writing deliberate works of fantasy, yet somehow the experience of it comes as a complete surprise to each new victim.

Tolkien himself was one of the early victims, so that for many years, the kind of critics who had never been to Elfland, and prided themselves on not knowing the place, would point sneeringly at the mere length of *The Lord of the Rings* as if that alone were sufficient proof that it was egregiously padded. For some reason or other, they did not say the same thing about *Anthony Adverse* or *War and Peace,* both of which are much the same length, nor even about the 4,215 back-breaking pages of *A la recherche du temps perdu.* There is some padding in the earlier parts of *The Fellowship of the Ring,* to be sure; some of the verses could be cut, and some of the 'hobbit-talk', and probably the whole business of Tom Bombadil; but the second and third volumes are tightly plotted and could hardly be reduced without fatal damage to the story.

And yet the padding in those early chapters is there; there was more of it in the first few drafts; and strange to say, Tolkien put it in deliberately. The unexpected success of *The Hobbit* led his publisher (and readers) to clamour for 'more about Hobbits'; he complied only reluctantly and with

misgivings. Two months after beginning 'the new Hobbit', he wrote to
C. A. Furth:

> The Hobbit sequel is still where it was, and I have only the
> vaguest notions of how to proceed. Not ever intending any se-
> quel, I fear I squandered all my favourite 'motifs' and charac-
> ters on the original 'Hobbit'.

With no clear idea what the sequel should be about or where it was
going, Tolkien threw in all sorts of odd ingredients. He knew very well
that he was making stone soup, and was not about to reject any idea that
would help him keep the story moving and pad it out to a suitable length.
Tom Bombadil had first appeared in the *Oxford Magazine*, unconnected
with Hobbits and Middle-earth; but he could be made to fit, so into the
pot he went. Then there were Barrow-wights and Black Riders and other
adventures by the way, and the inn at Bree (a spontaneous invention),
where Tolkien found a mysterious Hobbit with wooden shoes, nick-
named 'Trotter': the first faint origin of the character that would eventually be revealed as Aragorn. The soup was already getting rather full of
herbs and seasonings, but it still needed *meat* – a principal ingredient to
supply the stock and unite all the other things into a harmonious whole.

One day, the 'meat' came to Tolkien in a flash of insight. Bilbo's magic
ring was not just a stock fairy-tale ring of invisibility; it was *the* ring, the
One Ring that ruled all the others, and Sauron (who had already appeared in several unpublished stories) was trying desperately to find it.
At the Council of Elrond, which seems to have been a process of discovery and decision for the author as much as for the characters, it came out
(after several drafts) that the only way to defeat Sauron was to destroy
the Ring. That was the unifying device Tolkien needed – the meat for the
soup – and from that moment, it was stone soup no longer. But he had
already dragged in so many ideas and characters and complications that
it could not all be worked out quickly.

Up to this point Tolkien, like the Englishman in our local legend, had
only been climbing the first high ridge beyond the fort, in the mistaken

belief that the mountains were immediately beyond it. With the discovery of the One Ring, he saw for the first time a wide stretch of country that he had to traverse before reaching the true foothills; and disappointed but not daunted, he plodded on. Five years after he began 'the new Hobbit', he informed Stanley Unwin with naive and touching faith:

> It is now approaching completion. I hope to get a little free time this vacation, and might hope to finish it off early next year.... It has reached Chapter XXXI and will require at least six more to finish.

In fact Chapter XXXI was 'Flotsam and Jetsam' – Book III, chapter 9 in the published epic; just about halfway through *The Two Towers*. There were in fact another thirty-one chapters to go. Since Rohan and Gondor, the War of the Ring, and Gollum (not yet 'tamed') had already been introduced to the tale, it is hard to imagine how Tolkien could have thought that he would finish it all in just six. But there was Mount Doom – so clear, so tantalizingly close! He could not accept, could not perhaps even imagine, that it would take seven more years of struggle and revision before he brought the story to its conclusion. He had set out to take a morning constitutional, and ended by making the journey of a lifetime.

The Lord of the Rings has been the great exemplar (and fatal temptation) of every writer of epic fantasy since; and we might suppose that subsequent writers in the field would have learnt this along with its other lessons. We would be disappointed. One writer after another has set out to write a long-form fantasy tale, and grossly underestimated the size of the task and the length of the finished work. In one of his moments of wisdom, David Eddings observed that a man who has never walked a mile on his own legs has no clear idea how far a mile is. It seems that a writer who has never written a trilogy has no clear idea what a trilogy is, either. To judge how long a story will have to be, it appears, you have to have personal experience at writing stories of that size; and of course no one starts out with such experience.

In short stories and ordinary novels, this does not pose a problem. The novice writer has to finish his stories before he can hope to sell them; and with a finished text, a publisher always knows how far apart to put the covers of the book. But in fantasy especially, writers routinely sign publishing contracts for long series when only the first volume (or none at all) has been completed. The rest of the series is a gigantic promissory note, and many a writer has found himself bankrupted by the compound interest on his own projected tale.

Tad Williams is one of these. His first long epic, *Memory, Sorrow, and Thorn,* was sold to DAW Books as a trilogy, and duly published as such. *The Dragonbone Chair* is a hefty book, but it delivers exactly what Williams and his publisher called for – the first third of the story, as projected at the time. *The Stone of Farewell* is much the same size; but it becomes increasingly apparent by the end of that book that the story is not two-thirds done. *To Green Angel Tower,* as a result, is a monster. DAW was just able to publish it in hardcover as a single volume of over 1,000 pages, though it had to be set in smaller type to fit in one binding. It would have been about 1,600 pages in paperback, which is considerably more than a mass-market binding can hold together. So DAW was reduced to the rather ludicrous expedient of releasing the paperback as a two-volume volume – *To Green Angel Tower, Part 1* and *To Green Angel Tower, Part 2.*

Wiser heads might have surrendered to the inevitable a little sooner and with better grace, and divided the oversized third volume in two from the outset. Then at least each volume would have had its own title, instead of the third and fourth books sharing one title between them. Williams and DAW did just that with his next series, *Otherland,* which also proved too long for the originally projected three books. His recent *Shadowmarch* series repeats the procedure. Indeed, it would not be unfair to describe Tad Williams as a professional writer of four-volume trilogies.

The real master criminals of Aggravated Trilogy, however, were yet to come. The late Robert Jordan originally planned *The Wheel of Time* as a tightly-plotted six-book series, which, even so, would have been the largest epic fantasy yet conceived and written as a single story. In the event,

Jordan died after finishing eleven books (plus a prequel), leaving notes for the twelfth and last; and *that* book turned out to be so long that it had to be divided into three. The result, after nearly thirty years' work by two authors, was a sheer monstrosity, a soap opera sprawling over fifteen fat volumes, to a total length of more than four million words.

Those four million words, I am afraid, contain a great deal of deliberate padding. I have heard, in such a way as to believe it, that Jordan was asked by his publisher, Tom Doherty, and his editor/wife, Harriet McDougal, to stretch the series out to more volumes and so exploit its huge commercial success. Certainly a lot of his readers felt exploited. Customers' reviews of the middle volumes on Amazon.com make amusing reading. From about the fifth volume on, there begin to be large numbers of one-star reviews, increasingly strident and despondent, complaining that the story is being drawn out with pointless detail and needlessly elaborated subplots, and that each book brings the main plot no closer to a conclusion. There are endless descriptions of characters' clothing, and where the clothing was made, and by whom, and when; and endless scenes of the hero's various mistresses conspiring together, or against one another, and being spanked, a particular Jordan specialty; and of subordinate characters making tea, drinking tea, gossiping over tea, and in at least one case, being poisoned by tea. Adam Roberts, in his wittily scathing review of the series, has described the cumulative effect as 'epic Miss Marple'.

By the eighth book, these readers are saying openly that they have been swindled, that they are swearing off Jordan and will not waste any more of their money on a series that will evidently never end. Yet many of the same people returned to the series, as the dog returns to his vomit, only to make the same complaints about volumes nine, ten, and eleven. Sad to say, the news of Jordan's death, and the hiring of Brandon Sanderson to finish the series, actually gave these long-suffering customers a new feeling of hope – a feeling that the tale actually *would* be finished, that at long last Doherty and McDougal would bid its swelling expanse be stayed and swell no further. The first book under Sanderson's byline did not much encourage this hope. *The Gathering Storm* was a fine title for the first volume in Churchill's monumental history of the Second

World War; it is rather less fine as the title of the *twelfth* volume in a series. One might reasonably expect that the storm would be well and truly gathered by then.

Since then, the crown, if we may call it that, has passed on to George R. R. Martin. *A Song of Ice and Fire* was always intended to be a large work, but it, too, has grown in the telling. With more than the usual effrontery, Martin dealt with the proliferation of subplots and the slowing of forward momentum simply by *fission:* he divided the enormous cast of viewpoint characters into two sets, and dealt with them alternately, so that the fourth and fifth books in the series cover the same span of time in different parts of the map. Whether he will get a grip on the reins again in the remaining volumes, or let the horse have its head and go galloping off in all directions for the rest of his days, is still an open question. I have met Mr. Martin once or twice, and I met Robert Jordan once, and in each case I had the strong impression that I was not talking to a well person. If Martin were to follow Jordan's descent into the void, and die with his *magnum opus* still unfinished, I would be saddened but not, I fear, surprised. At present he plans to finish the series in seven books, a plan, he says, that is firm 'until I decide not to be firm'. Perhaps it will be his great good fortune to die in harness at the age of 105, still scribbling away at the twenty-fourth and final (we mean it this time) book of the series.

In less flagrant cases, the growth can be contained short of metastasis; that is, without subdividing the story into more books. J. K. Rowling handled the Harry Potter series in this way. The first three books are neat little novels of the size that publishers used to prefer for juvenile books. After that, Rowling got on more slowly; the drafts grew longer, and because readers by the million were clamouring for each successive book, her publishers developed a distressing habit of wrestling the first draft out of her grip as soon as it was finished and publishing it more or less unedited. The later books would have benefited a good deal from judicious cutting; but the publishers calculated (quite correctly) that they would sell in boatloads without it, and did not propose to delay the releases for editorial work that was not *commercially* necessary. As a result, the Harry Potter books make a very odd-looking set on a shelf: three thin books followed by four increasingly fat ones. This posed a severe puzzle for the filmmakers, who finally had to deal with the sprawl of *The Deathly Hallows* by dividing it into two films: the Tad Williams method again.

The cumulative effect of all this is to make it seem that epic fantasy writers are by nature sprawling, slovenly, and self-indulgent. Some are, no doubt, but most are defeated by the nature of the medium – and of human experience. You set out to write an epic, and figure out what the story will be about, and who the heroes are, and what kinds of places you want to visit along the way; and you divide your outline into roughly equal thirds, and expect to write a trilogy. But the story has an exasperating way of growing bigger as you go along. The mountain that you chose for your destination turns out to be twice the size you originally thought, and consequently, twice as far away; and having travelled two-thirds of the distance you planned for, you find you are only one-third of the way there. Then, if your series has been a commercial success so far, you may find your publisher happily playing along, encouraging you to spin it out into as many books as they can profitably sell. If not, you are liable to be dropped in mid-series and never reach the destination at all.

Once you have completed one of these epic journeys, you will know in your muscles and your bones how long the journey is, and how much the real distance exceeds the apparent distance; and the next time you make such a journey, you can go forewarned. So Tad Williams discovered that what looked (to him) like three volumes would reliably turn out to be four, and he has learnt to pack an extra lunch. But if you set out on a journey the size of Jordan's, you may not live long enough to profit by the lesson. The only person who knows in his bones how a six-book journey turns into fifteen is Jordan, and his bones are lying in the graveyard and will not make any more journeys now.

I do not know of any general solution to this problem; perhaps no general solution is possible. The tragedy of life, they say, is that it takes a whole lifetime to learn how to live. That tragedy is doubled for travellers in Elfland: the elves are immortal, but the travellers are not. And just as, in the old tales, a mortal man could spend one night with the elves to find that a hundred years had passed in the outside world, a fantasy writer can easily spend the best years of his working life covering a few fleeting days in the history of his invented world.

If there is a solution, it will demand a quality that our ancestors valued highly, but that we have almost forgotten: they used to call it *wisdom*. It is truly said that fools learn by experience; wise men learn by watching fools – and by taking to heart the rules and maxims that other wise men have distilled from the experience of fools. Perhaps there is some rule or maxim that a wise man could devise to solve the paradox of epic fantasy, as there is (nowadays) a rule for solving the rather similar paradox of motion, first presented by Zeno of Elea.

One form of Zeno's paradox explains that it is impossible, from any starting-point A, to reach a fixed destination Z. To get there, you first have to get to point B, halfway between A and Z. But then you have to get to point C, which is halfway between B and Z; and so on. By the time you reach point X, which is halfway between W and Z, you will be heartily cursing the name of Zeno and wishing you had never set out on such an impossible journey. Or if your name is Newton or Leibniz, you will notice that each stage of the journey takes only half as long as the last, until you are adding up an infinite number of infinitesimals. Then you will pause to catch your breath and invent calculus, add up all the infinitesimals, and reach Z in a finite time.

The wisdom that could solve the paradox of epic fantasy may likewise be a matter of mathematics. What we want is a formula that will tell us, as a general rule, how much longer the actual story is likely to be compared to the outlined or projected story. Tad Williams worked out a solution for his own special case: if it looks like three books, it will actually take four. Extrapolating this to cover other situations is the tricky part, and that problem has not yet been solved. Of course, even with a general solution, we would still need the wisdom and the will to do what it prescribes. That is, I think, largely a matter of *courage*: it means having the guts to wrap up a successful series while the readers are still calling for more, instead of spinning it out to greater and greater lengths for easy profit. It means trusting our talent and our skill – knowing that if we can finish this one tale, the Muse will not desert us; there will be other tales to tell, and if we choose the best one available, our audience will follow us there.

Elfland is large, and those who have once visited it nearly always want to return. We need to put our trust in that; and we need the wisdom to measure our journeys in proportion to our writing lives. As long as writers lack that wisdom and that trust, they are likely to go on making journeys that never seem to reach their destinations, but merely peter out, defeated by the paradox of Zeno's mountains.

QUAKERS IN SPAIN

Prose style is an endless source trouble for writers in the imaginative genres, and fantasy above all. There is always the temptation to write in an entirely modern, journalistic style. Such a style is like an Interstate highway in America: smooth, fast, easy to travel, with no dangerous or distracting bumps. The drawback is that you can drive from coast to coast without ever really seeing anything but the road itself. Such styles and such roads are good for getting to your destination in a hurry. But experienced tourists, and experienced readers, find it more fun to take the scenic route.

If you are a writer of some ambition, then, you will try to build a scenic route with your prose. Ursula K. Le Guin's superb essay, 'From Elfland to Poughkeepsie,' is all about this difficult art. It has every virtue, alas, except that of being in print. It used to be collected in *The Language of the Night,* which I strongly recommend, if you can manage to buy, beg, or borrow a copy. If not, you and I will have to worry along together the best we can.

As Le Guin says, what you want in imaginative writing, and in fantasy particularly, is *distancing from the ordinary.* The scenic route had better show the reader some scenery that she will not see in her daily commute. In fantasy, part of this effect is inherent in the subject-matter. A story about dragons is not likely to be mistaken for the morning newspaper.

But if you want to achieve the best effects, if you really want to sweep the reader off her feet and carry her into your imagined world, you need a style to match the substance. You will want to describe your freshly imagined world with fresh and imaginative language, or else you may put your reader to sleep with the very story that is meant to awaken her sense of wonder.

How, then, do you build a scenic route out of words? It is an easy trick to come up with a stilted and unnatural way of telling a story; and all you will achieve by it is to sound stilted and unnatural. The real trick is to come up with a style that is not quite like ordinary language: different enough to convey that this is another world, another culture, but ordinary enough that it does not get in the way of comprehension. The same technique has often been used to portray other countries and cultures in the real world; particularly, to give the flavour of a foreign language, with its own set of idioms and cultural assumptions, without actually writing in a foreign language.

Ernest Hemingway was an early master of this technique, but also an early failure; oddly enough, his failures came after his successes. While still in his twenties, he perfected an entirely new narrative prose style, an etiolated strain of which has become the default 'transparent' style of the modern American novelist. Of all the bizarre experimental styles of the 1920s, from Joyce's glossolalia to Stein's commaphobia, Hemingway's was the only experiment that really succeeded. It doesn't matter; he paid the rent for them all. Unfortunately, he soon degenerated into self-parody. A man's wit may outlive his wits, in which case he will retain the ability to write arch imitations of his best work long after time and tide and whiskey have washed away the rest of his talents.

Alas, Hemingway's judgement went the way of his skill, for the style he chose to imitate in his parodic senescence was not the style of the successful experiment. It was the laboured and mannered style of *For Whom the Bell Tolls*, the purpose of which is to make you think that the book has been translated from Spanish with painful literalness. So he peppered his prose with irrelevant Spanish *palabras* that you are expected to know the meaning of, not because they have no English equivalents, but because, you know, people speaking Spanish occasionally throw in a really *really* Spanish word just to remind you that they are not speaking English or Cantonese. He also makes much use of Spanish idioms translated word for word, no import how unnaturally the sentence puts itself in consequence. He makes sure, once in a while, after giving you a phrase in English, to repeat himself in Spanish, *y relanzarse en castellano*. And he uses *thou* and *thee* with wild inconsistency, often forgetting and settling for *you*, and just as often using *thee* as the nominative case – an error that he probably picked up from the Quakers. Quakers in Spain, forsooth! There are words in Spanish for people who do this kind of thing, and we do not have such words in English, but I will not instruct you in obscenity by repeating them here. *Sinvergüenza* is one of the milder ones.

The effect of all this is to persuade you that the book you are reading was written by an idiot savant who is intimately acquainted with foreign idioms, but does not know how to form English contractions. In a short book, like *The Old Man and the Sea*, it is just tolerable, but at greater length, or done inexpertly by other hands, it descends rapidly into schtick.

There is a place for this technique, but not much of one. It is appropriate to dialogue, not *récit*, and at that, to the speech of characters who are either represented as speaking a foreign language (to the narrator, that is), or as foreigners trying to speak the narrator's language with imperfect success. A little goes a long way. It is particularly unsuitable for long passages when the subtextual 'foreign' language is itself fictitious. Tolkien skirted the bounds with his gobbets of undigested Elvish, but at least his Elves, when speaking English, spoke English (a peculiarly archaic and cadenced English, which suited them, and sorted well with the things they had to say) and not a tortured attempt at Elf-glish.

A variation on this is the faux archaism one finds all too often in fantasy. Archaic words and turns of speech can create that distance from the ordinary; but 'like bicycling and computer programming', as Le Guin says, you have to know how to do it. An archaic style has to be built from the ground up; and since nobody *speaks* archaic literary English nowadays, it has to be built up from encyclopaedic reading. Two twentieth-century fantasy writers did this perfectly: E. R. Eddison and Lord Dunsany. If you want to see how they did it, and what effects can be achieved in setting the tone for a fantasy by language alone, I recommend that you read Eddison's *The Worm Ouroboros* and Dunsany's *The King of Elfland's Daughter*. (I rejoice to report that *Ouroboros* has been made available in an ebook edition for just one U.S. dollar.)

But if you don't do the trick perfectly, you risk losing the knowledgeable reader; and if you try to fake it, you might as well not do it at all. Bad archaism takes us straight to that other fantasy world (they call it Hollywood), where Tony Curtis made himself a laughingstock by saying in a thick Bronx accent, 'Yonder lies de castle of my fodda.' In fact, Curtis never said any such thing; the story originated with Debbie Reynolds, who was misquoting one of his lines from *Son of Ali Baba*, with the full and malicious intention, I am afraid, of making him look like a fool. But the butchered version of the line became instantly famous, and still gets a knowing snigger from fantasy fans, and from people who think they are film buffs. Don't set yourself up to be the butt of such a joke. Unlike Tony Curtis, you might actually deserve it.

If you insist on rejecting this excellent advice, you can fadge up your 'archaic' dialogue the way David Eddings did in *The Belgariad*. Just take a completely modern, colloquial, slovenly speaking style, and do a global search-and-replace to swap in three or four archaic-sounding words. The worst example I have ever seen was on a store-front sign, advertising 'Ye Olde Video Shoppe' – the perfect place for all those people who wanted to rent authentic 16th-century films. Eddings' technique was not much better. This is a random, but not unrepresentative, sample from *Castle of Wizardry*:

> 'Food hath been prepared, your Majesty,' Mandorallen assured him. 'Our Asturian brothers have provided goodly numbers of the king's deer – doubtless obtained lawfully – though I chose not to investigate that too closely.'

It is not the language of a hero, even a minor hero, but of a cop on the take in a 1970s TV drama. Change *hath* back into *has,* and *goodly numbers* back into *a lot* or *plenty,* and *doubtless* back into *no doubt,* and you have expunged every trace of archaic English. As Le Guin says, 'You can't clip Pegasus' wings that easily – not if he has wings.' Mandorallen's dialogue is simply a fake, a cheap knockoff ordered straight from Ye Olde Baloney Factory.

So what's wrong with baloney? In this case, it wastes words, and it does nothing to convey the idea that Mandorallen comes from a different culture. If you are going to make people talk strangely in a book, whether they are Spaniards in *For Whom the Bell Tolls* or Arendish knights in a cheapjack epic fantasy, there ought to be a *cultural* reason for them to do it. The cultural value of archaic English was described admirably by J. R. R. Tolkien:

> Real archaic English is far more *terse* than modern; also many of the things said could not be said in our slack and often frivolous idiom.

Mandorallen has the slack and frivolous modern idiom, with just enough archaic words sprinkled in to make it ludicrous. But then, Mandorallen himself is ludicrous, and is probably meant to be. Eddings dresses him up in the trappings of European chivalry, without understanding them in the slightest. They are either used as window-dressing, or brought in to make the characters look like fools. Everybody is summarily judged by the mores of middle-class America *circa* 1980, and everybody is found guilty, except the ingenue hero and his utterly spoilt love interest; those two never come into conflict with modern American culture, because they have as nearly as possible no culture at all.

In Eddings' world, noblemen like Mandorallen spout highfalutin language about courtesy and courage and knightly duty, while starving their peasants to death and grinding their faces in the dust. Why? Because that's just what noblemen do: ask any Connecticut Yankee. The idea that chivalry was *real,* that there were men who tried to live up to the highfalu-tin sentiments, is not even entertained as a falsehood.

To make doubly sure that his character will seem a complete block-head, Eddings puts him in a country whose borders are fixed by the gods. There have been no wars except civil wars, no invasions, no *reason* to have a caste of mounted warriors or a feudal society, for the last five hundred years. Mandorallen's old-fashioned ideals and old-fashioned language are put in the story for no better reason than to make him ridiculous. And that is a poor reason to put anything in a story, unless the story is a delib-erate farce. *The Belgariad* is only an accidental farce. But I shall have more to say about that later.

GWLADYS AND THE GHRAEM'LAN

I f prose style in fantasy is fraught with peril, *naming* is a plain old-fashioned minefield. Fantasy writers have a tendency to throw together names from any and all sources that strike their fancy, without thinking how such disparate words came to be in the same language together, or even in the same world. Writers who are very good at other aspects of their craft can still inexplicably fall down in this one area. I am sorry to make a bad example of my friend Jonathan Moeller, but when I first began to read his *Demonsouled* series, and the first two characters I met were called Mazael and Gerald, I was thrown out of the story long enough to cry aloud to the unheeding night: 'Mazael is good; Mazael is right and proper. There ought to be a fantasy hero named Mazael, and now, thank God, there is one. But why on earth is he hanging out with someone whose name is a foreign monstrosity like *Gerald?'* In Le Guin's terms, Mazael is from Elfland and Gerald is from Poughkeepsie, and there needs to be some explanation of how they ever came to meet.

There are two bad ways of coming up with fantasy names; or rather, of the many bad ways that one could devise, two are much more popular than the rest. One is to name people and places with the kind of jumble one might get by rolling Perquackey dice. This will do for a joke, or for a private diversion like a role-playing game: a friend of mine once did yeoman service with a character unfortunately named Hogheospox. But it is unkind to inflict such names on the reading public; especially *your* public.

The opposite error is the perfectly mundane name with a coat of bad paint. I am referring to the practice, which perhaps originated in cheesy Gothic romances but is most firmly established in bad fantasy, of taking familiar or (God help us) transiently fashionable names, changing a couple of letters, sticking in an apostrophe or two, and passing them off as something wild and exotic. It never works. You cannot pass off pinchbeck as fairy-gold, especially to the fairies.

Women writers seem especially prone to this fault – Anne McCaffrey and Katharine Kurtz, with their hordes of imitators, come quickest to mind – which is not surprising, since this is also one of the stock methods of coming up with 'different' first names for girl children. P.G. Wodehouse hit it exactly in 'The Spot of Art'. His Gwladys Pendlebury was not Welsh, which would have been an adequate excuse for the W in her forename; she was a pretentious *artiste* from a posh part of London, and as English as toad in the hole. Bertie Wooster's aunt spotted the danger at once:

> 'You sit there and tell me you haven't enough sense to steer clear of a girl who calls herself Gwladys? Listen, Bertie,' said Aunt Dahlia earnestly, 'I'm an older woman than you are – well, you know what I mean – and I can tell you a thing or two. And one of them is that no good can come of association with anything labelled Gwladys or Ysobel or Ethyl or Mabelle or Kathryn. But particularly Gwladys.'

Of course, there are male offenders as well, and they make up in volume of prose whatever they lack in numbers. Robert Jordan's names are cringingly awful. Take *Rand al'Thor*: evidently the name of a Dutchman who was named after a Norse god by Arabs, if internal evidence is anything to go by. *Trollocs* is a bad enough word, reminding one irresistibly of *trollops* as well as *troll-orcs*, but nothing compared to the ghastly names of their tribes: *Ahf'frait, Al'ghol, Bhan'sheen, Dha'vol, Dhai'mon, Dhjin'nen, Ghar'ghael, Ghob'hlin, Gho'hlem, Ghraem'lan, Ko'bal, Kno'mon.* A man who can perpetrate a travesty like that, and deliberately put it into print, should not have the freedom of the streets. He embarrasses the human race by ass'hoh'shieh'shun.

But let us give this dha'vol his dh'ue. Jordan may be the worst offender in bulk, but it is Terry Brooks who holds the record for the worst single name ever used in a fantasy novel: the unforgettable Allanon. (I keep wondering when his sidekick Allateen will show up.) Gary Gygax's city of Stoink is a dismally close second.

George R. R. Martin, though a much better writer than Brooks or Jordan, comes perilously close to the Gwladys standard here and there in *A Song of Ice and Fire.* Some of his names (Tyrion, Daenerys, Arya) are quite effective, if over-freighted with the letter Y. But they sort very ill with the not-quite-English names like Eddard and Samwell, and those in turn clash just perceptibly with straight English names like Robert and Jon. One gets the feeling that Martin knows what he is trying to do, but hasn't a sufficiently developed ear to tell when he has done it. His names go in and out of tune; or rather, they seem to be playing about three different tunes at once, and the tunes don't harmonize.

In all of sf and fantasy, there have been three authors who perfectly mastered the delicate art of nomenclature: Tolkien, Cordwainer Smith, and Mervyn Peake. Tolkien, of course, worked for decades at his invented languages, and the names he coined in those languages are both euphonious (unless he intended them not to be, like 'lovely Lugbúrz') and authentic. But he was also deeply versed in English names, both of people and places, a study that would well reward many writers who do not trouble themselves to undertake it.

As for Smith and Peake, between them they cornered the market in Gothic bizarreries, which happened to perfectly suit the kinds of stories they wanted to tell. It is perfectly correct that Lord Jestocost of the Instrumentality should keep a cat-descended mistress called C'Mell. The C stands for Cat, you see; it is a natural contraction, like the one you occasionally used to see for Scottish names – MacLeod reduced to M'Leod, as it is in one of Kipling's stories. What's more, Smith actually unbends far enough to explain this. The average perpetrator of Aggravated Apostrophe couldn't explain *why* she sticks pothooks in the middle of words, not to save her life, her soul, and her poetic licence. Or at any rate, she doesn't bother.

Likewise, it is only right and just that the nemesis of Sepulchrave Groan, Earl of Gormenghast, should be called Steerpike, and that he should apprentice for a time under an old medico by the name of Prunesquallor. (It is still more right and just that the medico should have a ghastly sister named Irma Prunesquallor.) These names are English, or something near it, but so cleanly transported out of the normal conventions of English naming that they take on some of the glamour of names like Aragorn and Lúthien. And unlike Tolkien's names, it is possible to work out something of their meanings, or at least associations, without an unobtainable dictionary of an imaginary language. This is a great timesaver.

An honourable mention – I owe this observation to my friend John C. Wright – should go to David Lindsay, for some of the names in his infinitely strange novel, *Voyage to Arcturus*. Despite the name and the ostensible setting, this book really belongs to the genre of fictionalized philosophical declamations, like *Atlas Shrugged,* rather than science fiction or fantasy as such; which is one of the reasons why it has gone out of vogue, and (frequently) out of print. But Lindsay must have been a considerable influence on Smith and Peake, with his protagonist Maskull, and characters with names like Krag and Nightspore. These names are not all euphonious and certainly not all of one linguistic type, but they are striking and evocative, and that makes up for some of their deficiencies.

Lindsay's onomastic triumphs, known to thousands who have never read any of his books, are *jale* and *ulfire,* the two primary colours that one sees in the Arcturian sunlight, but never on earth. Those names are so suggestive that I can almost imagine what they look like. Jale, to me, suggests a colour between red and green that is nevertheless *not* yellow;

pale like milky jade (for all I know, the name may be a portmanteau of *jade* and *pale*), but as bright and vivid as any colour you can see through a prism. (I have read that women with the recessive gene for colour-blindness sometimes report seeing such a red-green colour, but I don't know what it looks like to them.) Ulfire suggests a torridly brilliant colour somewhere beyond violet, which would affect the human eye somewhat like the purplish-white of the very hottest lightning. Lindsay describes ulfire as 'wild and painful', and jale as 'dreamlike, feverish, and voluptuous'. I can well imagine those descriptions fitting with colours of the sort I have described, though I came up with those impressions from the words alone, without ever having read any part of the book. The names are just that magnificently evocative.

Each method has much to recommend it, but for a writer in a hurry, with middling linguistic gifts, I would recommend leaning towards the Smith-Peake school. Inventing languages, like writing archaic English (or, as Le Guin says, bicycling and computer programming), is one of those things you have got to know how to do before you can do it. Few fantasy writers are inclined to take this advice, alas; and so the Ghraem'lans, I fear, will be with us for a long time to come.

TYRION 13:4

Most readers like *formed* stories; I have this taste to an unusual degree. I have never lost, or as the sophisticates would call it, 'outgrown' the taste for a well-turned plot that I drank in – not with my mother's milk, for I was raised on cheap commercial substitutes – but at any rate with the oldest stratum of my father's teaching, with the earliest books (after Dr. Seuss) that he gave me to read. A child is not subtle; a child likes stories to be marked by clear signposts, and would rather have five spoilers than one ambiguity.

Partly this is because a child has not formed a pattern of expectations about stories. Grown people dislike spoilers, I suspect, largely because they have read (or watched) so much fiction that they generally know what to expect: a real surprise, to them, is a rare and precious thing, and if you deprive them of one, you do them a real injury. *Every* turn in a story is a surprise to a child, and the suspense can become too hard to bear. It was a master-stroke when William Goldman, in the film version of *The Princess Bride*, had the grandfather interrupt his telling of the tale to reassure his grandson that Buttercup 'does not get eaten by eels at this time'. To an experienced reader, any peril that threatens to kill off the heroine a third of the way through the book is an obvious bluff. A very young reader has to find out the hard way.

Nowadays, even the average six-year-old has imbibed enough stories, chiefly through the medium of television, to be wise to the obvious tricks; in sad consequence, even a six-year-old may be angry at spoilers. But there are less naked ways to signal the phases of a story, ways that can be made subtle enough (and misleading enough) to please the palate even of a very old and sophisticated reader. One of the best devices for this purpose is the chapter break, with or without a title.

Some readers profess to be indifferent to chapters in fiction, and some, I believe, honestly are. (Sherwood Smith has told me that she is one.) I have written elsewhere about the difference between analytic and immersive reading. Some people read so immersively that they sweep right past analytic details like chapter breaks. They are so entranced by the picture that they do not even notice the frame. But as Chesterton said, the frame is an integral part of the picture; the vision is no vision at all unless it is limited. The human eye and the human brain are not capable of seeing everything at once; we have to look at particular things in order to see anything. Chapters are framing devices; they signal to us, 'Here is a particular vision; here is a thing for you to look at.' A chapter does not stand alone, but it presents an object for separate consideration, and invites you to pause for thought, to integrate that object into your understanding of the whole subject, before you move on to the next bit. *Selah.*

This is obviously useful in non-fiction, and even the most immersive reader is liable to be flummoxed by (say) a fat reference manual with no chapters or table of contents. But it is useful in fiction as well; I would even say it is a minor art in itself. At any rate I think it is worth looking at some of the principal functions of chapters, and the ways they can be used effectively or badly. If you will bear with me, I shall deal with this matter in my own way: by telling a story about it:

Among the ancient Greeks, the fundamental unit of literature was the βιβλος or 'book', by which they meant a single papyrus or parchment scroll. These scrolls were mass-produced in more or less standard lengths; a regular-sized scroll held about 20,000 words in the handwriting of a trained scribe. Writing to this length became a standard skill expected of all authors. If you wanted to write something longer, you had to break it up into several books; and then, if you were at all clever, you made a virtue of necessity by taking up a different part of your subject in each book. You would divide your *opus* into as many topics as the number of books it would fill.

Often, though, you would find yourself dealing with topics too small for a 20,000-word book. In that case, you would put several topics together in one scroll, and to help your readers find their way, you would introduce each new topic with a heading. The word for heading is κεφάλαιος in Greek, *capitulum* in Latin, *chapitre* in Old French – hence the English word *chapter*.

This was useful for more things than just subdividing topics. There were no pages in a scroll, and no two copies were ever exactly alike; so the only good way to point to a specific passage in a book was to cite the chapter it occurred in. This ability was so spectacularly useful to scholars that they began putting chapter breaks into *all* their books, even those that dealt with one topic in an unbroken chunk of text. In such cases they would not trouble to name the chapters, but only number them, just as we number the pages in printed books. Often these arbitrary chapters were as short as a page in a printed book, or shorter; so you could give quite accurate citations by this method.

With the advent of printing, it became possible to use page numbers for this purpose, and by the twentieth century it was an academic *faux pas* to give references by anything *but* page number. But in the last few years we have come full circle: the mass-produced printed book, with the same text on page 43 of every copy, is slowly giving way to the electronic book, in which 'page 43' is defined on the fly by the amount of text that happens to fit on your particular screen in your preferred font size. Some learned publications are already falling back on chapter references for citations in recent books. Indeed, this has become the *de facto* standard in citing authors like Dickens or Tolkien. Their books have been reprinted in so many different editions that references by page number are virtually useless. You can say the same of ebooks, with the 'virtually' left out.

An ebook reader ordinarily saves your place in a book; even with printed books, you can use bookmarks or dog-ear the pages. But these methods are not infallible. Most recreational readers have no need to make citations to a text, but we have all had the experience of losing our place in a book. Numbered chapters are about the best tool ever invented for dealing with this difficulty. I think it safe to say that this is a basic function of chapters: if a book has chapters at all, we can reasonably expect them to do that much.

The other main function of chapters, referred to earlier, is to identify topics within a book. This is a plain necessity in most kinds of non-fiction; in fiction it is a luxury, but often a useful one. Chapter titles can help the story along by building expectations, like 'Slavery and Escape', from *Robinson Crusoe*. They can help to set a mood, like 'The Shadow of the Past', from *The Lord of the Rings*. A real virtuoso like Dickens can even use *fictitious* chapter titles to give us the feeling of having read an entirely imaginary book. This is from *Our Mutual Friend:*

> 'This, sir,' replied Silas, adjusting his spectacles, and referring to the title-page, 'is Merryweather's *Lives and Anecdotes of Misers*. Mr Venus, would you make yourself useful and draw the candles a little nearer, sir?' This to have a special opportunity of bestowing a stare upon his comrade.
>
> 'Which of 'em have you got in that lot?' asked Mr Boffin. 'Can you find out pretty easy?'
>
> 'Well, sir,' replied Silas, turning to the table of contents and slowly fluttering the leaves of the book, 'I should say they must be pretty well all here, sir; here's a large assortment, sir; my eye catches John Overs, sir, John Little, sir, Dick Jarrel, John Elwes, the Reverend Mr Jones of Blewbury, Vulture Hopkins, Daniel Dancer—'
>
> 'Give us Dancer, Wegg,' said Mr Boffin.
>
> With another stare at his comrade, Silas sought and found the place.

'Page a hundred and nine, Mr Boffin. Chapter eight. Contents of chapter, "His birth and estate. His garments and outward appearance. Miss Dancer and her feminine graces. The Miser's Mansion. The finding of a treasure. The Story of the Mutton Pies. A Miser's Idea of Death. Bob, the Miser's cur. Griffiths and his Master. How to turn a penny. A substitute for a Fire. The Advantages of keeping a Snuff-box. The Miser dies without a Shirt. The Treasures of a Dunghill—"'

'Eh? What's that?' demanded Mr Boffin.

' "The Treasures," sir,' repeated Silas, reading very distinctly, ' "of a Dunghill." '

The best chapter titles at once set up our expectations and play with them; they are just misleading enough, or incomplete enough, or vague enough, to excite our curiosity without spoiling the surprise. Dickens knew this technique forwards and backwards, and 'The Treasures of a Dunghill' is, by this standard, a brilliant title for a chapter. The phrase is, on the face of it, an oxymoron; we trust that the author means something clever by it; but *what*? We read on all the more eagerly to find out, as we do after finding a clue in a mystery novel.

At their best, chapter titles can heighten tension in much the same way as prophecies. Indeed, the two techniques can be combined. Stephen R. Donaldson did just that in *White Gold Wielder*, the sixth Thomas Covenant book. Lord Foul, the villain, has prophesied that Covenant will freely and voluntarily give him his magic ring, the white gold of the title, to the ultimate ruin of the Land; and by this time we know that Lord Foul's prophecies, as a rule, really do come true. It gives us a feeling of honest jeopardy, and ramps up the tension. As Covenant journeys towards his final confrontation with Foul, Donaldson heightens the sense of dread and fatality with chapter titles like 'The Last Bourne', 'Enactors of Desecration', and 'No Other Way'. These little flourishes emphasize the mood without giving any clue how, or whether, Covenant can escape his prophesied doom and save the Land.

This is a difficult art, and it is not surprising that in a subsequent series, his space opera *The Gap*, Donaldson gave up and did without chapter titles altogether. Unfortunately, he flew to the opposite extreme, to the detriment of his work and the confusion of readers: he adopted a system that does not fulfil *any* of the usual purposes of chapters. This method has since caught on; George R. R. Martin made it famous (or infamous) in his monster epic, *A Song of Ice and Fire*. Martin, it would seem, borrowed the device from Donaldson; Donaldson may have got it from Asimov, who used something like it in *The Robots of Dawn*; Dorothy L. Sayers did the same sort of thing in *Five Red Herrings*. Beyond that, the pedigree becomes obscure.

The system I am referring to is this: to introduce each chapter, not with a title or even a number, but simply with the name of the point of view character for that section of the text. The author simply slaps a name at the top of a fresh page, followed by that character's inmost thoughts and experiences in gruelling detail, until it comes time to interrupt the story with a cliffhanger and go haring off after the next victim.

Now, this is not a bad idea in itself. It does take rather a lot of work to come up with titles like 'The Treasures of a Dunghill' or 'The Shadow of the Past', and still more to ensure that they help the story along without acting as spoilers. If it will ease a writer's passage through this vale of tears to call his chapters 'Tyrion' or 'Angus' or 'Daneel', or even 'Jim-Bob' or 'Hey, you!', he can do it with my blessing. But Donaldson and Martin, especially Martin, use it in a confusing and self-defeating way.

To begin with, they don't *number* their chapters. This is a serious offence against the reader, particularly in the size of the books in which they are doing it. If I am reading an 800-page doorstop, a task I do not routinely accomplish at a single sitting, I want a foolproof method of remembering my place in case the bookmark falls out between times. For this purpose, as I said above, chapter numbers are the perfect *aide-mémoire*. Chapter *titles*, without numbers, can be unhelpfully hard to find when the book (like most novels) has no table of contents.

When there are twenty-three chapters with the same name, and not even the dignity of a Roman numeral to tell t'other from which, Madness beckons from its twitchy horse and takes me for a gallop. I could fairly easily find my way back to Jon IV, or Jon X, or Jon CLXXVI, *Dei gratia capitulum*, but Messrs. D. & M. do not accord me even that exiguous courtesy. There is no way to tell one 'Jon' chapter from another at a glance. The only thing for it is to pick a likely-looking chapter at about the right place in the book, read a bit of it, and then cast backwards or forwards a chapter at a time until I find where I last left off. And that is not foolproof, for I often find the characters agonizing over the death of somebody who was alive and well when last I saw him, and wonder if I have missed a crucial stretch after all.

This brings me to the other defect of this method, which is not intrinsic to the method itself, but is so often associated with it that I wonder whether they are really separable. Authors, it seems, do not commonly name their chapters after their viewpoint characters unless those characters come in regiments and battalions. I once counted all the POV characters in *A Song of Ice and Fire;* I believe I lost count somewhere around three thousand, but my memory may be at fault. Probably it was more. The result of this is that a character's story arc will be interrupted in mid-scene with a glorious cliffhanger, well worthy of the old *Doctor Who* at its cheesy best, and then nothing more will be heard of him for two or three hundred pages.

In the later books, Martin took to driving his characters in two sets abreast, so that some of the cliffhangers in the third volume are not taken up again until the fifth. There comes a point at which mere suspension of disbelief is no longer enough. What is wanted is suspension of *memory,* and it takes a steel cable of Verrazano-Narrows gauge to carry the load. It was this, more than any other fault (except the infamous 'Red Wedding'), that caused me to give up on *ASOIAF* after three volumes.

Yet one seems to get very little meat out of this method, no matter how much the plotline of these books resembles something filmed in an abattoir. For once we have caught up with Pauline still in her peril of a thousand pages ago by our time, or two hours ago by hers, and see her suitably extricated, we are then obliged to sit down and listen while she soliloquizes about what all the *other* characters are doing, and where they are now, and whether they can be counted on to have done what they set out to do, and whether they are dead or only shamming.

There is a certain amount of this in many good books. *The Lord of the Rings* derives great poignancy from the constant uncertainty of Frodo's position, as Aragorn and Gandalf and the rest strive superhumanly to perform heroic deeds that will be wasted if Sauron recovers the Ring. But there are only eight (surviving) members of the Quest, not eighty, and they do not *all* sit around between battles and wonder what all the other seventy-nine are up to. In both *The Gap* and *ASOIAF*, the enormously complicated plots are largely driven by groups and knots and claques of characters trying to second-guess each other, and generally getting it wrong.

There must be a better way to construct a five-volume novel, and there certainly are better ways to maintain narrative tension. But both Donaldson and Martin appear to have become inebriated with the exuberance of their own ingenuity, as well as verbosity. Their books would be shorter, neater, and more effective if they could resist the temptation to chase up side-issues and minor characters in the same detail as the deeds of their principal heroes. They set out to be architects, but spend most of their time and skill carving gargoyles for their drains. The least they could do is have a table of contents, and put numbers on the gargoyles.

TEACHING PEGASUS TO CRAWL

As I said earlier, the choice of an appropriate prose style for a fantasy tale is a decision fraught with peril. We are tempted to choose a style that will convey the proper sense of wonder and adventure, and the air of old times and alien cultures; or would, if we only had the skill to pull it off. If we lack that skill, our stories will sound rather like an untrained singer trying to do the lead in *Rigoletto* – ambitious, but inept. And this will get us laughed at.

It is safe to say that none of us enjoy being laughed at. So for perhaps forty years past, there has been a reaction in the opposite direction; and I am afraid that is an even worse error. The sensible reaction would be to learn how to produce the effects that we wanted; the real reaction, for far too many writers, has been simply to give up trying and settle for a bland quotidian style. Their stories are inept without being ambitious. And this is worse, for unless they are very lucky, it gets them ignored and forgotten. They may truly be hearing the horns of Elfland in their heads; but they cannot play that music. What they do play is a tuneless mishmash compounded of slovenly description, spin-doctoring, and rhetorical fog.

Most of what I could say about this has been said with magnificent wit and force in 'From Elfland to Poughkeepsie', which I referred to earlier. The language of fantasy should be appropriate to fantasy; the speech of heroes should be heroic; the sound of the lame excuse should not be heard in that land. This is the law and the prophets: all else is gloss. But I should like to dwell upon the gloss awhile, as the fantasy field has changed enormously since 'Poughkeepsie' was published, and by no means all for the better.

After some preliminary rumblings, the field of fantasy became a real commercial genre very suddenly. I have written about the Fantasy Big Bang of 1977, when the field as we know it emerged full-grown, swinging a sword and swashing a buckler, from the dog-eared notebooks of the late J. R. R. Tolkien. This is an exaggeration, but not a very gross one. Besides *The Silmarillion,* that year marked the appearance of three first novels and a film that permanently changed the commercial and critical climate in fantasy publishing.

It also marked the official annexation of Elfland by Poughkeepsie, though the elves have been fighting a valiant rearguard action in the remoter parts of the country. In short, 1977 was when Fantasyland opened for business at its present location. And one of the signal qualities of Fantasyland is the utterly pedestrian tone of its prose. Some fantasy authors are simply inept with language, which would have disqualified them in the old days; others, alas, have quite deliberately stripped all the magic and grandeur out of their writing, coldly and deliberately, to make the newcomers from suburbia feel perfectly at home.

In Northrop Frye's taxonomy, as propounded in *Anatomy of Criticism,* the plots and characters of fantasy normally occupy the levels of Romance and High Mimesis, with occasional excursions into Myth. But from 1977 on, it became usual to write their stories, and still worse their dialogue, in the ordinary novelistic language of Low Mimesis and Irony. The strain is too much for the structure to bear. Where Aragorn and Gandalf, or Eddison's four Lords of Demonland, spoke like heroes and behaved accordingly, too many of their successors come across as over-aged adolescents playing at knights and dragons. It is no calumny to say that the tone of the average commercial fantasy novel nowadays is not much above the tone of the average Dungeons & Dragons campaign. This is no accident, for D&D players are the most identifiable and exploitable demographic for fantasy publishers.

I have played a lot of D&D in my time, as it happens, and what I observe time and again is players who Just Don't Get It. They are ostensibly playing heroes, or at least quasi-heroic adventurers, but they give these characters a kind of life that betrays their utter unfamiliarity with either heroism or adventure. Some time ago, I dabbled in Third Edition D&D after an absence of many years. One party in which I participated was, or rather played, a group of irregulars in the service of a baron whose domain was beset by ogres, pirates, and assorted menaces from the omnium gatherum of the *Monster Manual*. The Dungeon Master was an ex-serviceman, familiar with the bureaucratic organization of modern armies, and utterly ignorant of the deeply personal and emotional loyalties that characterized the feudal system. Though we were, sword for sword, the most valuable retainers the baron had, we were never actually permitted to meet him, and seldom even saw the captain of his men-at-arms. We were dealt with summarily by a mere lieutenant, briefed, debriefed, conferred with in map-rooms, and generally treated with less courtesy and ceremony than a mediaeval king would have shown to the merest beggar. Kings touched commoners for the king's evil, but our lord the baron did not touch commoners at all. Corporate Poughkeepsie, with its disgusting rudeness and indifference, and the layers of insulation built up to protect every person of importance or even self-importance from the importunities of the public, was in full possession of an ostensible fortress of Elfland.

All this showed in our DM's use of language, which I shall mercifully spare you; and the like attitude, with much less excuse, shows daily in the pages of modern commercial fantasy.

At about this point in her argument, Ms. Le Guin gave some more or less random examples of dialogue in great works of fantasy, and one less great. I should like to offer some beginnings, since that is where the modern, groomed, workshopped author is taught to display his very finest wares:

When Mr. Bilbo Baggins of Bag End announced that he would shortly be celebrating his eleventy-first birthday with a party of special magnificence, there was much talk and excitement in Hobbiton.

Bilbo was very rich and very peculiar, and had been the wonder of the Shire for sixty years, ever since his remarkable disappearance and unexpected return. The riches he had brought back from his travels had now become a local legend, and it was popularly believed, whatever the old folk might say, that the Hill at Bag End was full of tunnels stuffed with treasure. And if that was not enough for fame, there was also his prolonged vigour to marvel at. Time wore on, but it seemed to have little effect on Mr. Baggins. At ninety he was much the same as at fifty. At ninety-nine they began to call him *well-preserved*; but *unchanged* would have been nearer the mark. There were some that shook their heads and thought this was too much of a good thing; it seemed unfair that anyone should possess (apparently) perpetual youth as well as (reputedly) inexhaustible wealth.

'It will have to be paid for,' they said. 'It isn't natural, and trouble will come of it!'

This is Tolkien's version of Poughkeepsie, but already in the distance we can hear the horns of Elfland tuning for their first fanfare. The events described are entirely pedestrian, a birthday party and some small-town gossip, but they are fraught with significance. In a way, the entire plot of *The Lord of the Rings* is merely the rigorous and complete exploration of the 'trouble' that came from Bilbo's 'unfair' lease of youth and riches.

Note that Tolkien, whose literary influences were nearly all dead before 1900, is not at all afraid to begin with sixty years of backstory, pithily summarized, or to burden the reader with *récit* instead of a cinematic 'teaser'. This is how such things were normally done in the days when literature was not deformed by the perceived need (and impossible desire) to compete with television on television's home ground. I believe that we shall yet see a return of the *novelistic* novel, as opposed to the novel that tries to be a faithful replica of an unmade movie. But that is not, generally speaking, what we are getting at present:

> The sun was already sinking into the deep green of the hills to the west of the valley, the red and gray-pink of its shadows touching the corners of the land, when Flick Ohmsford began his descent. The trail stretched out unevenly down the northern slope, winding through the huge boulders which studded the rugged terrain in massive clumps, disappearing into the thick forests of the lowlands to reappear in brief glimpses in small clearings and thinning spaces of woodland. Flick followed the familiar trail with his eyes as he trudged wearily along, his light pack slung loosely over one shoulder. His broad, windburned face bore a set, placid look, and only the wide gray eyes revealed the restless energy that burned beneath the calm exterior.

That is the opening paragraph of *The Sword of Shannara,* one of the Big Bang fantasies of 1977. Or rather, it is part of the opening paragraph, for we are treated to several more lines of visual description of the mysterious Mr. Ohmsford. Although Brooks's first novel has been mercilessly derided as a mere pastiche of *The Lord of the Rings,* it is in fact something very much more (and less): a *translation* of LOTR from epic English into modern pedestrian novelese. It is the Fantasyland version of Tolkien.

See how the story opens with an attempt at cinematic description. Everything is seen through the camera eye, beginning with a long establishing shot of the countryside, then closing in on the weary figure trudging through the landscape, ending with an extreme closeup focused tightly on the eyes. It is true that everything is seen as through a gel filter, darkly, for Brooks's descriptive powers are not great, and if we form a vivid image of a countryside from these vague cues, it redounds to our credit and not his. 'Touching the corners of the land' is strictly meaningless, as nasty a bit of mock-poetic trumpery as you could hope to find among the sham beams of a Tudor pub in Peoria. The bit about the restless energy revealed by Flick's wide gray eyes is simply a cheat, and a cheat of a particular kind that I should like to discuss in more detail.

For this is the very essence of the Fantasyland style: to swaddle the reader in visual description, engaging her mind (I assume a female reader for convenience' sake, as the writer I am dissecting is male) in the mild trance state most conducive to escapist reading, while communicating the real gist of the matter in windy abstractions. Nobody could possibly see restless energy burning in a man's eyes as he trudges wearily down a hillside trail, even if there were somebody there to look for it. (There is not; Flick is alone at this point, except for the omnipresent camera eye.) What we have is a purely subjective and fanciful opinion about Flick's character, passed off as physical description and therefore as fact. If a *character* formed such an impression of Flick's eyes, the reader would know where she stands. She would know it was an opinion, no more reliable or well-informed than the person who made it, and from this she could learn not only about Flick but about his observer, and the relationship between them. As it stands, she learns only that Terry Brooks wants her to think of Flick as a dynamo of hidden energies, without showing him doing anything remotely energetic, let alone dynamic.

Le Guin observed that a fantasy writer's true quality shows best in his dialogue. It takes three full pages of Flick's solo trudgery before we come to the first line of dialogue in the story:

> The dark figure was almost on top of the Valeman before Flick sensed its presence looming up before him like a great, black stone which threatened to crush his smaller being. With a startled cry of fear he leaped aside, his pack falling to the path with a crash of metal, and his left hand whipped out the long, thin dagger at his waist. Even as he crouched to defend himself, he was stayed by a commanding arm raised above the figure before him and a strong, yet reassuring voice that spoke out quickly.

'Wait a moment, friend. I'm no enemy and have no wish to harm you. I merely seek directions and would be grateful if you could show me the proper path.'

When two strangers cross paths in a wood, and one wishes to ask the other for directions, he does not customarily introduce himself by sneaking up within arm's length and doing his best impression of a Black Rider. No indeed: accosting the other man from a distance and asking the way to Poughkeepsie is the generally accepted thing. It's a fake scare, followed by fake reassurance. Again we have the cloudy attempts at description ('great, black stone'), merely to give the author a plausible defence against the charge of 'telling, not showing'. And again the meat of the matter, such as it is, is told and not shown, an opinion enforced by pure auctorial fiat. 'A strong, yet reassuring voice' could sound like anything. We are told that Flick was reassured by it, but we really have no idea why.

By the bye, at this point, four pages into *The Sword of Shannara*, we have got considerably less distance with the story than Tolkien took us with the three short paragraphs that begin *The Lord of the Rings*. The Fantasyland writer is nothing if not verbose.

Another of the Big Bang fantasies was *Circle of Light*, by Niel Hancock. It is difficult today to believe that Hancock's overgrown fairytale was highly acclaimed in its day and sold over a million copies. It is very much a book of the Seventies, and you can hear deliberate echoes of *Jonathan Livingston Seagull* in the opening:

> On the morning of his leaving, he erased all his tracks from that part of heaven, carefully stacked new star branches in a neat pile behind the entrance in the dark mouth of the universe, and sadly began the thousand-year trip down the side of the sky that closely resembled a large mountain. If you looked at it that way. If you didn't, it might seem very much like walking out your own front door and down the steps.

It is an accomplishment, I suppose, to be both twee and portentous at the same time, but that combination is Hancock's speciality. Our unnamed character is a Bear, *the* Bear in fact, a stock anthropomorphic fairytale Bear of the sort that has been familiar to everyone since Robert Southey seeded Elfland with three of the species; but he is also the reincarnation of an ancient hero. So we are told in the subsequent pages, though we never learn just what he did that was so heroic that it would still be remembered in the twilight of the ages. Again we see this curious tendency to show trivialities and baldly tell (or even omit) essentials. In this case, it is overlaid with a New Age mystical conceit, for the Bear's journey is, of course, his reincarnation to fight the good fight once more. The tone is more juvenile than that of *Shannara,* but the cinematic pretensions and windy vagueness are much the same.

Now, I do not mean to give the impression that a cinematic, novelistic technique (derived, by the way, from Hemingway's successful experiment referred to earlier) is *always* inappropriate for fantasy. Special circumstances can justify it, as in the third of the Big Bang novels:

> She came out of the store just in time to see her young son playing on the sidewalk directly in the path of the gray, gaunt man who strode down the center of the walk like a mechanical derelict. For an instant, her heart quailed. Then she jumped forward, gripped her son by the arm, snatched him out of harm's way.
>
> The man went by without turning his head. As his back moved away from her, she hissed at it, "Go away! Get out of here! You ought to be ashamed!"
>
> Thomas Covenant's stride went on, as unfaltering as clockwork that had been wound to the hilt for just this purpose. But to himself he responded, *Ashamed? Ashamed?* His face contorted in a wild grimace. *Beware! Outcast unclean!*

Stephen R. Donaldson, by his own admission, is a notorious over-writer, but there are no wasted words here. Nothing is spent on the setting, beyond the mention of the store and sidewalk; we recognize this as a street zoned commercial, part of our own world. We have immediate action, immediate conflict, and are faced at once with an urgent question. Why is Thomas Covenant subjected to such execration merely for walking down the street? What ought he to be ashamed of? Just as Bilbo's neighbours adumbrated the whole plot of LOTR in a sneering line of dialogue, the woman from the store (whom we never see again) sets up the essential conflict that drives *The Chronicles of Thomas Covenant the Unbeliever*. It is a powerful and engaging opening, though Covenant soon squanders the capital of sympathy that his author laid in for him. The action is described cinematically, if you like, but it is *action* and not impressionistic claptrap about the countryside. Like Tolkien, unlike Brooks and Hancock, Donaldson puts his subjective judgements where they properly belong, in the minds and mouths of characters who are capable of making those judgements *inside the story*. The narrator does not intrude at all.

But this exception, after all, works because Thomas Covenant really is a man from Poughkeepsie, or somewhere distressingly like it. The apparatus of the twentieth-century novel is appropriate to his tale, because he is a twentieth-century man, and his tale is about the head-on collision between Elfland and Poughkeepsie. Donaldson has described the *Covenant* books as a kind of inverse of *Idylls of the King*. Tennyson's masterpiece is the tale of how King Arthur was destroyed by a world full of petty and self-seeking men; Donaldson's debut is about a petty and self-seeking man who finds redemption in a world full of King Arthurs. The tone is often ironic, in Frye's usage of the term, because Covenant is an ironic hero. He speaks fluent Poughkeepsie, and the characters of the Land to which he is transported speak a highly idiosyncratic dialect pregnant with the unmistakable tones of Elfland.

One more example, and I shall leave the matter alone. This is not from the Big Bang, but from the monstrously long Fantasyland novel that fully assimilated and imitated all its predecessors. All the yardwork and busy-work, all the Extruded Book Product from the Old Baloney Factory, is summed up in this one encyclopaedic tale, and the beginning strikes the note with uncanny accuracy:

> The Wheel of Time turns, and Ages come and pass, leaving memories that become legend. Legend fades to myth, and even myth is long forgotten when the Age that gave it birth comes again. In one Age, called the Third Age by some, an Age yet to come, an Age long past, a wind rose in the Mountains of Mist. The wind was not the beginning. There are neither beginnings nor endings to the turning of the Wheel of Time. But it was *a* beginning.
>
> Born below the ever cloud-capped peaks that gave the mountains their name, the wind blew east, out across the Sand Hills, once the shore of a great ocean, before the Breaking of the World. Down it flailed into the Two Rivers, into the tangled forest called the Westwood, and beat at two men walking with a cart and horse down the rock-strewn track called the Quarry Road. For all that spring should have come a good month since, the wind carried an icy chill as if it would rather bear snow.
>
> Gusts plastered Rand al'Thor's cloak to his back, whipped the earth-colored wool around his legs, then streamed it out behind him. He wished his coat were heavier, or that he had worn an extra shirt. Half the time when he tried to tug the cloak back around him it caught on the quiver swinging at his hip. Trying to hold the cloak one-handed did not do much good anyway; he had his bow in the other, an arrow nocked and ready to draw.

This is Fantasyland in a nutshell. We have the cod philosophizing of Hancock, perhaps improved upon, certainly intensified, by the Liberal Application of Capital Letters. We have the blatant cribs from Tolkien, the Third Age and the Misty Mountains. We have a panoramic camera shot of some very unsatisfactory and out-of-focus scenery, the burden of which is simply the screenwriter's 'Exterior Fantasyland, day'. We do not yet, it is true, have any auctorial opinions about Rand al'Thor fobbed off on us as physical description, but we may confidently guess that we will not be deprived of that amenity for long.

Robert Jordan has rounded up all the usual suspects, and they all do exactly the Poughkeepsian duty that every right-thinking reader has learnt to expect. And he has done it without getting us any distance at all with the story. It takes him a full page to tell us that Rand's cloak is flapping in the wind. That may not be good writing, but at least it is an authentic sample of the long, slow slog to come. If nothing else, we can praise Jordan for truth in advertising. He has not only clipped Pegasus' wings, but broken his legs as well, and will spend the next ten thousand pages teaching him to crawl. It would be so unacceptably Elflandish to let him soar.

ALL HATS ARE GREY IN THE DARK

S o far in this book, I have dealt chiefly with points of style and
technique. Now I propose to change tack and take up some
points of subject matter. And first, because Sherwood Smith was
good enough to remind me of it, I shall deal first with a very common
fault that is all but guaranteed to knock me right out of a book: the villainous hero.

Now, I have no trouble with flawed heroes; I expect them, and rejoice
to see them overcome their flaws, or find ways to succeed in spite of them.
I can even find much to admire in anti-heroes. And I have patience with
ironic protagonists, the Yossarians and Babbitts and Humbert Humberts,
who are never represented as heroic in any way, and whose authors are
well content to portray them as the schnooks, schnorrers, and schlemiels
that they are. (How did we ever insult one another before Yiddish came
along?) What offends me violently is when a character is represented as a
Good and Upright and Virtuous Hero, when almost his every act betrays
him as a villain of the most heinous kind.

Consider the works of Mercedes Lackey and her horde of collabor-
ators. Lackey writes straightforward, button-pushing wish-fulfilment
fantasies aimed at the sort of adolescents who *feel* unbearably Special
and Unique and Misunderstood, but in fact are no better or more sensi-

DEATH CARRIES A CAMCORDER

tive than anyone else their age. She identified and saturated her target demographic of emo kids before emo had a name. Writing for such an audience, the temptation to lower the bar of heroism to the emo-kid level must be almost irresistible; at any rate, there seems to be precious little evidence that Ms. Lackey ever resisted it. She turned the 'Mary Sue' story into a commercial genre of its own.

I have, as it happens, only read one book by Lackey, *Magic's Pawn*. I am told that it is somewhat below her usual standard, but not unrepresentatively so. The so-called hero of this book is one Vanyel, a thoroughly spoilt teenage boy, a nobleman's son who is supposed to grow up a warrior and learn to defend his family's lands, but wants to be a musician instead. Instead of doing *anything* to make the best of a bad job, he constantly shirks every duty his father sets him, refuses even to learn one end of a sword from the other, and hides behind his mother's skirts to escape punishment.

So far, we have a good candidate for the title of anti-hero. In the terms of the three classic plot patterns, Vanyel has the makings of 'The Man Who Learned Better' in extraordinary abundance. But he is something worse than that. He combines an exceptionally thin skin with a total insensitivity to the feelings of others – not an uncommon combination in real life, but certainly not a heroic one either. One of the first scenes in the book shows him casually seducing a fifteen-year-old serving wench – not even out of appetite, but just because he is a rich pretty boy and feels that it is expected of him – then casting her aside out of sheer boredom, without the slightest regard for her feelings. In fact, he is rather carefully represented as wilfully unaware that she even has such things as feelings. From that point onward I positively hated Vanyel, and wanted him to die slowly of a loathsome disease whilst being lowered an inch at a time into boiling oil. But I was destined to be disappointed.

Instead, he is miraculously sprung from the fate-worse-than-death of doing his hereditary duty, and sent away to study to be a Herald Mage. He discovers that he is actually homosexual, a thing he had somehow never heard of before, despite his precocity in the matter of sexual experience. Lackey as much as tells us that this excuses his abominable behaviour to the serving wench, and indeed all of his other faults. Apparently homosexuality is a positive virtue in Lackey's world, for it causes its devotees to be unjustly persecuted, and we all know that anyone who has been unjustly persecuted is thereby immune to any criticism whatever. Or something like that.

So Vanyel immerses himself in Herald-Magery, despite having no discernible talent for the work, and a variety of tacky liaisons with men and other boys, playing roughly the part of a 'College Tart' at 'Wyvern', as C. S. Lewis called his public school in *Surprised by Joy*. And at the end, in the most disgusting *deus ex machina* I have ever read, he is struck by magical lightning and instantly receives every magical talent in the world at maximum intensity, fully trained and ready for use, together with the wisdom to employ them properly and heroically. And so the scene is set for the remaining books of the trilogy.

I threw the book against the wall so hard that I broke the wall. It didn't do the book much good, either, but at least the book was fortified by the hardness of Vanyel's heart and the thickness of his skull. This so-called hero had spent three hundred pages being a self-centred ass with all the charm of an ingrown toenail, and seemed to have learnt absolutely nothing from the knocks he took and richly deserved. Now all my hopes were dashed: I would never see him run over by a bus, lest his superhuman powers should damage the bus. But I think I have made my objections sufficiently clear.

Now to my principal *corpus vile*: the collected works of David Eddings, or, as he preferred to be called later in life, David-and-Leigh. (I am irresistibly reminded of *1066 and All That*, with its chapter 'King Williamandmary. England ruled by an Orange.') For the sake of chivalry and brevity, I shall ignore Mrs. Eddings' complicity in writing their early books, and refer to Eddings in the singular and masculine.

Eddings really was a man of one book, though he made a fat living for two decades by issuing it again and again under different titles and with different names for the characters. We have the ingenue hero, who either is a farmboy or (as Andrea Leistra points out) might as well be. We have the beautiful raven-haired sorceress, who takes the farmboy off on a quest for a magical blue stone. We have a landscape, or rather a mapscape (for an Eddings series ends only when every country on the map has been visited), stuffed full of amoral sidekicks and painfully incompetent villains for them to kill by the dozen. And when the quest succeeds, we have the inevitable boss-fight against Ultimate Evil, which the hero wins without breaking a sweat. That is the plot of the *Belgariad,* and the *Malloreon,* and the *Elenium,* and the *Tamuli,* and it made Eddings a wealthy man until the fashion changed in favour of 'grit' and 'edginess'. Then readers (or editors) began to demand that the heroes get beaten up in the process of saving the world, and even bleed a little now and then; and the sunny-side-up fantasies of Eddings lost some of their meretricious lustre.

Aside from their dreary repetitiveness, their really striking feature of Eddings' tales is the almost total absence of moral depth or insight. Let us consider *The Belgariad,* since it defined the template, and remains perhaps the best known of his works. Garion, the ostensible hero, is an adolescent country bumpkin without any character of his own, who (without ever seeming to learn much) gradually takes on colour from his older and worldlier companions. And what a lot they are!

We have Belgarath, the 7,000-year-old sorcerer, who was a petty thief as a boy and is one still, even though he could just as easily create things out of thin air as steal them. He is also a grave-robber, a murderer, and a superbly accomplished liar; but let us not flatter him unduly. Somewhere or other in the books, he says frankly that he prefers not to think in terms of Good and Evil, but merely of Us and Them. A franker admission of moral bankruptcy would be hard to find. If we plough right through the 1,200-odd pages of the *Belgariad,* we will find him living down to his principles in awful plenitude. He arbitrarily punishes one of the villains – Zedar the Apostate, who was Belgarath's friend, for whatever that may be worth, for ages and aeons before he turned his coat – by immuring him in the living rock for all eternity, *without killing him:* this for a simple manslaughter of the kind that Belgarath and Company have been performing in nearly every chapter. Within a few pages Zedar's victim is brought back to life, but a technicality like that is not enough to soften the carborundum heart of Belgarath, and he leaves Zedar to rot.

Polgara, his 3,000-year-old daughter, exhibits the maturity and self-control of a spoilt teenage drama queen. She delights to play the prim and proper lady, and apparently has never heard of sex, but she is a consummate cock-teaser and a master manipulator. She makes no effort to control her awesome temper, which she expresses in tantrums that wreck castles and cities, for which she never shows the least sign of remorse. That she should pay the damages, of course, is simply unthinkable. Her principal occupation is raising a line of small boys, the successive generations of her sister's descendants, whom she 'protects' from their ancient and implacable enemies by keeping them carefully swaddled in ignorance, illiteracy, and incapacity. She regularly loses her temper with Garion whenever he shows a generous impulse to others, or demands a morsel of truth from her.

These protagonists attract about the kind of followers you would expect. There is Barak, the Viking berserker, who counts his enemies by severed heads and has apparently never heard of negotiation. Hettar, who has the trappings of a Rider of Rohan gone very wrong indeed, has dedicated his life to the psychotic mission of committing genocide single-handed. Mandorallen is a stock mock-feudal aristocrat, ripe for the Jacquerie, the kind who knows nothing and cares less about the misery of the peasants who support him. (Such aristocrats did indeed exist. They were never common, except in rare and peculiar cases where they formed a class of absentee landlords, like the French nobility once gathered at Versailles, or the francized Russians of St. Petersburg. That the bloodiest revolutions in European history came to those two particular nations is no accident.) Mandorallen is also, by way of a hobby, a lifelong adulterer. The Princess Ce'Nedra is the world's most outrageously spoilt brat. She tries to enforce her will by gross emotional manipulation, and would be dangerous if she were any good at it. Relg is a bog-standard religious zealot, totally misconstruing the teachings of his God, with a pathological fear of human contact born of his exaggerated and Pharisaic notions of ritual purity. Silk, a.k.a. Prince Kheldar of Drasnia, is a thief, a spy, an assassin, a crooked merchant, a cheat at dice, and a wholesale purveyor of the finest gold-leaf filigree pathological lies. And so down the line.

Glenda Larke expresses her distaste for

> A mass of truly horrible characters none of whom I can empathise with, doing truly horrible stuff, none of which I can sympathise with. You've gotta offer me something better than that to keep me reading.

and

> Villains who have no purpose to their villainy except to be villainous. Why? What's the pay-off?

The payoff, dear lady, is that the villains exist to make the *other* horrible characters look virtuous and *sympathique* by contrast. They are the kettle for the pot to call black. Nowhere is this clearer than in Eddings. His principal villains are the Grolims, an improbably murderous priesthood whose sole religious function, as far as anyone can tell, is to perform wholesale human sacrifices in the Aztec style, carving out the victim's beating heart to burn it in a charcoal brazier. No matter what problem they are faced with, their inevitable solution is to make another sacrifice. This is intended to frighten their underlings into performing superhuman feats to propitiate the Grolims' wrath. It never works.

The Grolims also write their sacred scriptures on vellum made from human skin. Belgarath roundly curses them for this, not because it is wicked and wrong to murder human beings for leather, but merely because human skin won't hold ink. You would think that even a Grolim might have the intelligence to do his writing on a substance that *would* hold ink, that being the purpose of writing, but these are Eddings villains, whose malice is exceeded only by their stupidity.

Now, obviously a society infested with such rulers cannot endure. (The secular kings of Angarak are little better, besides being as superfluous as boils to a leper.) Not even the Aztecs were stupid enough to sacrifice their own people, or to arrange their horrific rites in a way so bizarrely reminiscent of the old management joke, 'The floggings will continue until morale improves.' Even so, the Aztec empire lasted only a few generations before going down to comprehensive defeat against a handful of Spanish adventurers. It existed by force and fear, and burst like a soap-bubble when force and fear were turned against it. But Eddings would have us believe that Angarak has been organized on these lines for thousands of years, going back even before Belgarath's time.

Of course there is only one reason for all this exaggerated awfulness. As long as Eddings' 'heroic' band of robbers, cutthroats, and bunco-steerers don't go performing human sacrifices and writing necromantic grimoires on dead bodies, they can excuse themselves for all the other evil that they do. And Eddings can pretend that he is writing about White Hats versus Black Hats, when in fact he is only dealing with two slightly different shades of soot.

This is an old game, but not as old as the ages. Nations at war have told stories about the atrocity of their enemies as long as there have been wars and nations. But it was not until the Boer War that governments systematically used stories of enemy atrocities to justify *their own* atrocities. The technique has since become a staple of wartime propaganda. If Boers bayoneted English children in the Transvaal, that made it all right for the English to lock up whole populations of Boers in concentration camps. If Belgian nuns were raped by the Kaiser's soldiers, then it was obviously correct for the Allies to use mustard gas on the Germans. Sometimes both sides in a war justified their own atrocities by attributing entirely invented ones to the other side – one of many practices that made the Spanish Civil War so peculiarly squalid. Even the Nazis had vestiges of conscience, which they could assuage by picturing themselves as Roland at Roncesvalles, defending Christendom against a godless horde. As it happened, Stalin's *apparatchiks* really were a godless horde, which made Dr. Goebbels' job easier; but that did not make the Nazis heroes.

Do we really want to set up the thugs of the SS as our standard of heroism? Eddings does not precisely do that, but given the context of mock-mediaeval fantasy, he comes as close as makes no difference. It stinks of moral cowardice and atrophied conscience. C. S. Lewis wrote in *Mere Christianity:*

> When a man is getting better he understands more and more clearly the evil that is still left in him. When a man is getting worse he understands his own badness less and less. A moderately bad man knows he is not very good: a thoroughly bad man thinks he is all right. This is common sense, really. You understand sleep when you are awake, not while you are sleeping. You can see mistakes in arithmetic when your mind is working properly: while you are making them you cannot see them. You can understand the nature of drunkenness when you are sober, not when you are drunk. Good people know about both good and evil: bad people do not know about either.

Eddings assigns his white hats and black hats almost at random, and expects us to accept this as a shorthand for heroism and a substitute for ethics. Now, ethics may not be all black and white, but if they mean anything at all, they are a matter of *lighter* and *darker;* and the Eddings method is very dark indeed. He could have saved himself the trouble of buying two colours of hats, though. All hats, like all cats, are grey in the dark.

SOCK PUPPET, SON OF SOCK PUPPET

B esides the villainous hero, there are several other ways to make a protagonist so unheroic that you rob him of his power to carry the plot. A frequent flaw is the so-called hero who has no character of his own, but exists as a mouth through which the author can make polemical speeches. John Galt's 70-page speech in *Atlas Shrugged* is the most infamous example, but sadly, far from unique. The hero as mouthpiece is a recurring phenomenon in science fiction and fantasy; and this sad phenomenon goes back to the very point at which the earlier forms of satire and romance first contributed their genes to that newfangled form, the novel.

We can find that point in the works of Jonathan Swift. Swift began as an old-fashioned satirist, but he borrowed the form of the novel from Defoe, along with the motif of the shipwrecked sailor; and into this vessel he poured all the venom and vitriol he had stored up against the human race. *Gulliver's Travels* began, perhaps, as a parody of *Robinson Crusoe;* but it is very much more than that. It is the first great work in English that is both a satire and a full-fledged novel; a case can be made that it is an early work of science fiction as well. The exploration of the New World and the Antipodes was on the cutting edge of science and discovery in Swift's time, just as the exploration of space was in the twentieth century. The little men of Lilliput and the big men of Brobdingnag, though invented as caricatures of mankind, were just within the bounds of plausibility according to the science of the day, just as H. G. Wells's Martians were in 1898.

Since the novel was a new art in Swift's time, and the satire a very old one, we should not be surprised that the satire in *Gulliver* is more consistent than the novelistic qualities. I mean no disrespect to Swift or his creation when I nominate, as the patron anti-saint of the 'mouthpiece' hero, Lemuel Gulliver himself. Gulliver does not have this flaw in the beginning. Swift introduces him as a master mariner, shrewd, level-headed, and profusely competent, just the sort of fellow you would bet on to make a good thing out of being shipwrecked. This is good and appropriate characterization, since it points up the contrast with the cunning but fundamentally stupid and mean-spirited Lilliputians. It is also the kind of characterization appropriate to a novel, rather than the flat and limited kind usual in pure satire. The Crusoe blood-line runs strongly in him.

In Book II, however, the miniature shoe is on the other foot, and Gulliver obediently turns into a bawling jingo nincompoop, bragging to the hugely superior King of Brobdingnag about the latest European technological marvels, and the efficiency with which Europeans can now competitively slaughter one another. This is necessary, if you like, because the whole point is to provoke the King into his famous outburst: 'I cannot but conclude the bulk of your natives to be the most pernicious race of little odious vermin that nature ever suffered to crawl upon the surface of the earth.' But it does not sort at all well with the character of Gulliver as previously established, and we begin to lose confidence in him and faith in Swift's intentions.

Book IV sees Gulliver suddenly converted to a more extreme misanthropy even than the King's. He becomes convinced that he and all his kind are no different from the loathsome Yahoos, and pines away for the superior goodness of the Houyhnhnms. In fact (and I believe this to be Swift's point), he has gone utterly mad. But it is an arbitrary madness. There is no particular reason why it should have happened to Gulliver; one would think, after all his experience of super-, sub-, and non-human intelligences and societies, that he of all men would be inured to the kind of shock that the Yahoos gave him. But Gulliver is nothing if not complaisant; he is quite willing to throw away sanity itself in the interest of his creator's polemic.

One might say that Gulliver's adventures ought to have happened to three different men, not one, at least if plausible characterization took precedence over brand recognition. Lemuel Gulliver is one of the very few fictitious characters who are known and instantly recognized the world over, putting him in a class with Sherlock Holmes, Don Quixote, and a few names from Shakespeare. But he is nearly always recognized as the Gulliver of Book I, the plucky sailor stranded in Lilliput. This is partly because so many people have met him either in pretty-pretty expurgated editions issued as children's books, which rarely extend beyond Book II and often stop after Book I, or through films which are still more drastically abridged. But it is still that first impression that persists, even among those who have read to the bitter end in the country of the Houyhnhnms. It is a testament to Swift's skill as a caricaturist that our first impression of Gulliver should be so vivid and lasting, incapable of being overwritten by any of the manifold changes Swift imposes upon him as he kicks the hapless mariner through the obstacle course of his philosophy.

Unfortunately for the rest of us, we are not Jonathan Swift or even Charles Dickens, another author whose excellence at caricature did much to mask his incapacity for character. When we lesser mortals try to make mouthpieces of our characters, the public can see our lips move, and this destroys the illusion. Fortunately, this in itself is not always a fatal flaw; but it is certainly not something one seeks as a reader. I, for one, tend to lose patience when the author violates his characters' integrity for the sake of his 'message'.

In our own literary ghetto, the author most infamous for this kind of ventriloquist work is, as James Blish dubbed him, 'Heinlein, son of Heinlein'. Blish, Alexei Panshin, and others have maintained that *all* Robert A. Heinlein's male protagonists (and some of the females) are merely idealized versions of himself, convenient mouths from which his *obiter dicta* can issue forth, thinly disguised as dialogue. There is some truth in this accusation; but it is not much of an accusation, at that, for the same could be said about any of us who write fiction. It is only in us that our characters live and move and have their being, and the range of their thoughts is at best limited to a subset of our own. Still, some characters are much more definitely author-identification figures than others, and some are much more damaged by their creators' experiments with brain-transplant surgery.

Why this should be so is, to me at least, an interesting question. I think the public image of Gulliver provides a useful clue. In Book I of *Gulliver's Travels*, Gulliver's character is perfectly integrated with his role in the story, and he can speak by his actions. In the other three books, his personality is deformed in various ways to serve as the author's stooge; but he has been well enough established that certain kinds of actions are obviously unsuitable for him, and so he has to stooge in words and leave the actions alone. He is not, for instance, sufficiently one of the 'little odious vermin' to make real trouble in Brobdingnag, which would probably get him squashed under a gigantic heel; but he can, while remaining Gulliver, sound off with the most idiotic cant about the supposed virtues of his countrymen. When a character is reduced to preaching what he cannot plausibly practice, that is a sure sign that something has gone wrong. It betrays a short circuit in the author's creative process.

Heinlein is universally acknowledged to be a preachy writer, but except in a few of his later and lazier books, he is nothing like the blathering egomaniac that his harsher critics make out. Most readers agree that his juveniles, and certain of his earlier adult novels, are his most successful works. There is plenty of preaching in, say, *Tunnel in the Sky* and *The Star Beast,* to take two of my own favourites; but it makes some difference who is doing it and why. Rod Walker is the unquestioned protagonist of *Tunnel,* but if any character in that book qualifies as 'Heinlein son of Heinlein', it is Deacon Matson. In most of Heinlein's successful books, there is a character whose principal function is to lecture the hero, and the success of the book tends to be in inverse proportion to the lecturer's actual importance to the plot. The 'Wise Old Man' is a staple of fiction, not, as Jung surmised, because he is a fixture of the racial unconscious, but because he is the handiest device on record for supplying needful exposition *in medias res*. Not even a maid and butler can outdo him.

On this hypothesis, where Heinlein went wrong in his later works was to let his heroes double as his mouthpieces, instead of separating the two roles. *Time Enough for Love* was the first important book in which the hero *was* the lecturer; consequently Lazarus Long was never given a forcible chance to shut up, and seldom had to *do* things instead of chattering. Other late Heinlein heroes and heroines had the same vice in varying degrees.

If all this is true, what about *Friday*?

Friday is the most interesting of Heinlein's late works, because it was (and was acclaimed for being) a partly successful return to his earlier style, while being written with a freedom and frankness that would have been unprintable in Heinlein's younger days. But it is only partly successful, and I blame that on the imperfect separation of roles. The lecturer in *Friday* is the Old Man, Kettle Belly Baldwin, who plays the part exactly as we would expect. But Friday herself goes in for a good deal of lecturing when Kettle Belly is not around, much to the detriment of the book. Consider —

At one point, Friday rockets off to New Zealand to be with her 'S group', the name Heinlein used in that book for the line marriages that were one of his many wet-dream alternatives to monogamy. Neither 'S groups' nor any other kind of large group marriage have ever been successful for any length of time, except when the dominant member of the group could physically or economically force the others to stay. I recall reading about an anthropologist who proposed to do his Ph.D. thesis on group marriages, and set out to study the long-term dynamics of a number of groups with an average of seven members each. Within a year, *every last one* of those groups had broken up in acrimony, and he abandoned his thesis.

But here we have Friday waxing lyrical about the benefits of a long-lasting eight-member group marriage, a subject quite beyond Heinlein's (or indeed anyone's) personal experience. She also goes on at some length about the suitability of such a marriage for child-rearing, another subject with which Heinlein had no experience. The difference is that many of his readers *did* have experience in bringing up children, and could see through him on that point, but hardly any could confute him on the other. Science fiction fans as a rule are a horny and antinomian lot, and inclined to buy into strange sexual arrangements for their fantasy value without investigating too closely into their plausibility. One 'Mistress Matisse' has published a Polyamory–English Dictionary, which contains gems like this:

> **Poly phrase:** 'The idea of line marriage has always appealed to me.'
>
> *English translation:* 'The idea of having sex with people younger than me has always appealed to me.'

The difficulty, of course, is that comparatively few of us want to have sex with people much older than we are. 'Line marriage', if it worked at all, would most often be a disguise for long-term prostitution, a newfangled way for rich older people to accumulate trophy spouses instead of rationing them out one at a time. It certainly would remain a rarity, if only because multiple marriages, like heavy atoms, are radioactive and tend to decay by emitting couples and alpha particles respectively. Above a certain size, they can hardly take on new members as fast as they lose the old ones, as our anthropologist friend found out. Definitely a specimen for the zoo of 'alternative lifestyles'.

For all this, Heinlein can be forgiven. A considerable part of his appeal comes from the fact that he was such an unapologetically dirty old man. But he is not content to present Friday's *ménage* as an ideal; he must kill two giants with one blow, not only Monogamy, but Racism as well. Friday's S-partners, who are open-minded and free-living enough to glibly undertake an eight-party marriage contract, are simultaneously shown as hidebound bigots of the most dated and embarrassing kind. A society that accepts marriages of eight people seems an unlikely candidate to disapprove of marriages between white New Zealanders and Maoris, or between whites and Pacific Islanders, but Friday's free-wheeling elder hippies do exactly that. In fact, the entire group breaks up over the shocking revelation that Friday is an Artificial Person, with exactly the kind of exaggerated revulsion that an over-macho heterosexual exhibits on finding that the girl he has just French-kissed is really a transvestite. We learn that Anita, the head of the *ménage*, has been a bully and an embezzler all along; this is meant to help explain the breakup – a thing that requires no explanation. What it does instead is make us further doubt Friday's sanity for getting herself mixed up in such a racket, and doubly doubt her paeans of praise for the 'S group' as an institution.

At this point I lose all belief in these characters, and am considerably disgusted with their author as well. He has tried to pour Hugh Hefner and Archie Bunker into the same skin, and there is simply no way to make them fit. Each of his points could be made separately, and lifelike, integrated characters could easily be devised to exemplify them; but they cannot be combined, not in this way. It is just too blatantly obvious that they are not acting from their own motives, but merely to act out the psychodrama that Heinlein's polemic requires. Friday is Heinlein's mouthpiece *for* line marriages, and so she swears by her hyper-extended family; she is also his mouthpiece *against* racism, and so she swears *at* them. It is difficult to do both at once, and Heinlein's attempt is thoroughly unconvincing.

And because all these contradictions are presented in a short space, no more than a quarter of a novel much shorter than *Gulliver*, the inconsistency is much more blatant than the slow and incremental vacillations of the unfortunate Lemuel. It nearly spoils what is otherwise the best of Heinlein's late novels, and might have ranked with his greatest works if he had been content to slaughter one sacred cow the less.

CAMPBELL'S CREAM OF FANTASY

By its nature, fantasy is supposed to be the literature of the unbridled imagination; all too often, the imagination is not only bridled, but blinkered and hobbled and confined to its stall in the barn. It is fairly usual for critics to call this process 'commercialization'; which is very odd, because the most commercially successful fantasies of all time have not been tamed or broken in this way. Rather, the breaking of fantasy is a *consequence* of its commercialization. Winged Pegasus will bear you with joy to the remotest reaches of Elfland, but he does not always come when you whistle for him. Poor old Dobbin, bridled, blinkered, hobbled, stabled, and without so much as a wish for wings of his own, can only take you for a weary plod round the paddock, but he is always at home and always pathetically grateful to be taken out for a ride. Pegasus is a rare beast, born of inspiration; Dobbins can be mass-produced.

Publishers will gladly commercialize a Tolkien, a Howard, or a Rowling if they can get one; if not, they will settle for anything that *looks* like fantasy, that exploits some of the same tropes and offers to scratch the same itch. The shop must remain open for business, come what may; and if the shelves are stocked with shoddy goods, that is better than no goods at all. Frederik Pohl has expressed the editorial dilemma perfectly: some stories you print with joy and thanksgiving; others, because the alternative is to put out a magazine (or a line of books) with a lot of blank pages. Unfortunately, the tendency of publishers, especially large conglomerates, is to see just how far they can adulterate their product line before it stops selling – how many times they can promise a flight on Pegasus and deliver a ride on Dobbin, before the audience gives up in disgust and stops buying tickets. And of course there is never any shortage of hack writers who will supply the Dobbin rides. Some of them know they fall short of their ideal, and some are blissfully ignorant; some would sell their own mothers to see their names in print, and some just want to make a living, and use hard work and elbow grease to eke out inadequate talent. They can surely be pardoned for their faults; but to pardon is not to approve.

The late Diana Wynne Jones, in her delightful *Tough Guide to Fantasyland,* wrote a brave and brilliant exposé of the various kinds of ersatz and shoddy with which the shelves in the fantasy section of the bookshop are kept artificially full. But her attack, for all its virtues, is aimed at superficial things; she never really addresses the question of *why* this tired stuff is written and sold. Of course the bookshops are cluttered with interchangeable products set in indistinguishable Fantasylands. But even when fantasy writers make an apparently honest effort to come up with original settings for their tales, the results often betray a disturbing imaginative penury. Ursula K. Le Guin had the right of the matter when she said, in 'From Elfland to Poughkeepsie':

> The general assumption is that, if there are dragons or hippogriffs in a book, or if it takes place in a vaguely Keltic or Near Eastern medieval setting, or if magic is done in it, then it's a fantasy. This is a mistake.
>
> … [A] writer may use all the trappings of fantasy without ever actually imagining anything.

But *having* the right is not the same as *being* right. Her definition of fantasy would exclude nine-tenths of the books with FANTASY in small lettering on the spines. Such a categorization is every bit as unhelpful as the attempts by John Grant and others to define fantasy in a way that excludes *The Lord of the Rings*. It is an exercise in locking the barn door when not only the horse but the very walls have gone.

We cannot now hope to exclude the cookie-cutter Fantasyland books from the category called 'fantasy'. But I will make so bold as to call them *failed* fantasy, in rather the same sense that the *Argonautica* could be called a failed epic, or *The Phantom Menace* a failed *Star Wars* prequel. The word *novel* has been defined as 'a book-length work of fiction that has something wrong with it', and in every art form failures far outnumber successes. There is no shame and little harm in having written a failed fantasy; but that does not place the failed work beyond the reach of criticism. Le Guin in 'Poughkeepsie' again:

> When you hear a new violinist, you do not compare him to the kid next door; you compare him to Stern and Heifetz. If he falls short, you will not blame him for it, but you will know what he falls short of. And if he is a real violinist, he knows it too. In art, "good enough" is not good enough.

Of course, some violinists and some writers fall short more than others. Some of those whose books are labelled 'fantasy' seem genuinely to believe that Fantasyland is 'good enough', and make no attempt to move beyond its trite conventions and faded scenery. Others don't even bother with that. They not only strip down their settings to the bare minimum, so that their characters seem to live in a vacuum, but praise themselves for doing so and heap scorn on the idiots who actually put effort into their settings. This is from a talk Terry Goodkind gave in 2000:

> The books I write are first of all novels, not fantasy, and that is deliberate; I'm really writing books about human beings. I believe that it's invalid and unethical to write fantasy for fantasy's sake, because fantasy for fantasy's sake is non-objective. If you have no human themes or values, then you have no life as a base value. Fantasy for fantasy's sake is therefore pointless.

At the other end of the spectrum from my writing are a kind of book that, for lack of a better word, I'll call 'world-building' – and I don't mean to disparage pure world building books for what they are: entertainment. I don't consider them valid novels.

. . . .

World-building to me is no better than holding up the drug dealer as an ideal because it is holding up as a normative value a world in which humans do not exercise volition, but instead is a history lesson of when this person was born 300 years ago and had 12 daughters with unpronounceable names who had offspring who went on to have this and that convoluted history, which may be entertaining, but is not a novel.

The contempt could scarcely be more obvious. And yet, at that time, Goodkind by his own admission had never read *The Lord of the Rings*. He considered it a 'world-building book' rather than a 'novel'. (The 'history lesson' sneer is a clear hit at all the detailed back-stories inspired by the Appendices of LOTR; *a fortiori* at the original, whether he was aware of it or not.)

But if *The Lord of the Rings* is about anything, it is about humans exercising volition. It is about power and renunciation, death and the desire for immortality, and coping with irreversible change. Those are 'human themes or values', or the word *human* has lost all meaning. According to Goodkind this cannot be so, because his particular brand of reductionism will not allow a book to accomplish more than one thing. He does pay lip-service to the idea of a range or continuum between 'pure novels' and 'pure world-building', but in fact he never speaks about anything but these two extremes, always heaping scorn upon the latter. If a book contains world-building, then it must leave something else out. That is like saying that a house with more than two bedrooms cannot have a kitchen. Houses are not all of a size, and neither are books. Tolkien's epic is roomy enough for both. Goodkind's books are also roomy, or at least they take up a great deal of space, but he fails to fit in more than the sketchiest strokes of setting.

The effect of this is very curious. I once saw a student production of *Richard III*, done without props, backdrops, or even costumes: not so much as swords for the fight scenes. (The cast wore monochrome tights of various hues, and consequently looked like a ballet class.) Nothing remained but the actors themselves, standing in various poses on a plain black stage and reciting speeches from Shakespeare. This made for a cheap production, a considerable virtue in the circumstances; and after all it was never billed as a professional performance.

Goodkind's books, however, *are* billed as professional work, indeed very highly touted by his publisher; and a book laden with scenery and descriptions of action is just as cheap to produce as one with nothing but dialogue. But *Wizard's First Rule* gave me just the same sense of talking heads in a void. Sometimes, as in the torture scenes, the action was described vividly enough to give me a clear picture of the character's entire body, and sometimes Goodkind's auctorial lantern shed enough light to illuminate a whole room; but not often.

The book contains a map, but it is hardly necessary, as there are really only three places of any consequence: the Westlands, the Midlands, and D'Hara. These countries are separated by nearly impenetrable magical barriers, and have evolved widely divergent cultures from a common origin in the time since the barriers went up. From this one would suppose that the barriers are aeons or at least centuries old. Not so: there are people not yet past middle age who remember when they were built. The world's history before that is an absolute blank. Nobody seems to have any memory or record of anything going back as much as a hundred years.

Similarly, we never are told much about how Darken Rahl came to power in D'Hara. In a way, this is a refreshing change from the Dark Lord who was Imprisoned in the Mountain by G'grizzwoz the Moonbat in the Eleventh Age of Bapfnir, and emerged after five Cycles of the Moon of Gormwit, *etc., etc.* Bogus detail is worse than none at all. But it does not inspire confidence when none of the older characters seem able to remember events from their own youth. We are all a product of our culture as much as of our genes, and it is a truism that characters in fiction are best realized when you can see how they interact with their habitat and history. But Goodkind's characters have a blank page for a habitat, and very nearly no history at all.

One step above no world-building, of course, is the terminally lazy kind. *The Belgariad* and its interminable rehashes make a fine example. Over *here* we have ~~Merrie England~~ Sendaria, and *there* are our stock ~~Romans~~ Tolnedrans, and *up yonder* are the ~~Vikings~~ Alorns, all portrayed with the careful realism of, say, a Benny Hill skit. The *Tough Guide* says nearly all that there is to say about these stock cultures, the Vestigial Empire and the Anglo-Saxon Cossacks and so forth; but Eddings goes the template one better, because every one of his characters conforms perfectly to the appropriate ethnic stereotype. Every Arend is fearsomely brave and blitheringly stupid, every Tolnedran is a money-hungry schemer, every Grolim is . . . well, a psychopathic serial killer. Subtle, that. Couple that with plots generated by tracing a path through every country on the map, and you have a recipe for highly commercial fantasy product which requires virtually no imagination at all.

Some authors are very industrious indeed in designing their settings, but their efforts are wasted because they pile detail on detail without ever thinking much about the fundamental assumptions underlying the whole work. One finds quite a lot of this in gaming tie-ins. Ed Greenwood's 'Forgotten Realms', even ignoring the material contributed by other hands, is an enormous feat of world-building, far larger in scope and detail than Tolkien's, and ought to be a masterpiece of its kind. But it falls short, because it is not based on any coherent vision of what a world could be like, but on the rules of *Dungeons & Dragons*.

The cultures of the Realms are a mishmash of colourful mediaeval, pseudo-mediaeval, ancient and Renaissance detail, systematically altered in the interest of modern political correctness. There are, for instance, no defined gender roles, virtually everyone is literate, and slavery is practised only by races and nations that are Evil with a capital E. This is revisionism with a vengeance, and the effect is made still odder by the casual racism that squats in the midst of it like – no, an elephant in the living-room is too commonplace – like a basilisk in a shopping mall. Greenwood gives us the titles and trappings of feudalism without the attitude of feudal loyalty, the intrigues of a Renaissance city-state without the economic constraints that made city-states viable, the impedimenta of ancient empires without the indifferent cruelty of ancient imperialism. It does not hang together. It is hardly intended to.

Now, as a setting for a game, this does not much matter. D&D was originally as artificial as chess: ill-assorted groups of 'adventurers', patterned vaguely after the Fellowship of the Ring, wandering through improbably spacious underground complexes excavated for no clear reason, practising aggravated assault and grand larceny on an omnium gatherum of exotic monsters. *Any* attempt at 'realism' is an advance on this in a way, and in another way it only shows up the silliness of the original conceit. The Palace of Versailles was built round a royal hunting-lodge, and takes much of its asymmetry and structural inconsequence from that. Well, D&D is like a palace built round one of those astoundingly tacky hot-dog stands in the shape of a giant hot dog. It is a brilliant testimony to the skill of the architects, but less creditable to their judgement.

Unfortunately, the bookshops over the years have been crowded with Forgotten Realms tie-ins, *Dragonlance* books, and other subliterary properties taking after these; and still more with fantasies not overtly related to D&D worlds, but in which one is never out of earshot of the rattle of polyhedral dice. A good many of the more ridiculous entries in the *Tough Guide* can only be explained genetically. The treatment of horses in failed fantasy, considered in its own right, makes no sense whatever. But when you reflect on the battalions of fantasy writers whose knowledge of equitation is chiefly derived from the overland movement tables in gaming rulebooks, you can see how something of that sort was bound to come about. To this day there are still younger writers who slavishly imitate the absurd conventions derived from role-playing games, just as there are writers who imitate the obvious and showy bits of Tolkien without ever having read his works.

Lowest of all are the chimaerical creations of the reckless genre-benders: the punk street elves, the samurai vampires, the Orcs in mirrorshades, who had their brief vogue in the 1990s, and mercifully failed to take over the whole ecology of Faërie. Suffice it to say that you cannot come up with a Good Idea for a fantasy story just by bunging together two tropes pulled out of a hat. Brian Aldiss says that his best ideas come from the intersection of two ideas, but not *any* two ideas: his ideas come in pairs of a particular kind, one 'exotic', one 'familiar' (in his usage of the words). Stephen R. Donaldson reports the same phenomenon; so can I, for what that may be worth. But if you cross and re-cross exotic specimens without ever going back to the familiar for fresh genetic material, the resulting hybrid will almost always be sterile. It may not even survive being decanted from the test tube. Fantasy works by juxtaposing the strange and the familiar, so causing us to look at the familiar with fresh eyes. A landscape composed entirely of the bizarre is not fantasy but dada.

I should, however, mention some of the many honourable exceptions. Guy Gavriel Kay does brilliant work with well-researched and well-drawn analogues of historical settings. Susanna Clarke has mined a vein all of her own, rich but narrow: part English folklore, part Regency novel. China Miéville and his fellow-travellers have built bizarre Victorian Gothic structures that owe little to the gingerbread castles of commercial fantasy, though I don't care for the relentless nihilism that informs their work. And there have always been those like Poul Anderson, Mary Renault, Lloyd Alexander, and Evangeline Walton, who went back to the myths and legends of many cultures and produced their own strikingly original variations on those themes.

Tolkien used to talk of putting real people and historical events into the Pot of Story until they became part of the Soup. Easily nine tenths of the fantasy books on the shelves are of no interest to me, because a slight glance through them reveals that nothing has been added to the Pot except the leftovers of yesterday's meal. The Soup has become a factory product: Campbell's Cream of Fantasy. All we need now is Andy Warhol to do the cover art.

THE LEADEN RULE

The process that replaces winged Pegasus with plodding Dobbin, and Tolkien's 'Soup' of myth and legend with 'Campbell's Cream of Fantasy', does not stop with debasing settings and motifs. It debases *themes* as well. The old folktales, among many other things, were wisdom literature, a thing that does not exist in any thoroughly modern society. We have a number of authors nowadays who want to create a substitute for wisdom literature; what they actually do is write books with titles like 'The Rules of X' or 'Chicken Soup for the Y'. Not having much in the way of wisdom themselves, they substitute pop psychology and bumper-sticker slogans.

This is bad enough in the modern world; it is doubly bad in fantasy, for it is false to the whole atmosphere of Faërie. Heinlein expressed a useful rule in *Magic, Inc.:* whereas the physical world is subject to unalterable physical law, the 'Half World' of magic and spirits (a name I have swiped for my own use) is a place where anything is *physically* possible, but *morally* and *metaphysically,* everything is subject to 'the Customs', which are as unalterable in that world as gravitation is in ours. In this, Heinlein showed a better understanding of Faërie than hundreds of fantasy writers since. G. K. Chesterton drew the same distinction in different terms:

It might be stated this way. There are certain sequences or developments (cases of one thing following another), which are, in the true sense of the word, reasonable. They are, in the true sense of the word, necessary. Such are mathematical and merely logical sequences. We in fairyland (who are the most reasonable of all creatures) admit that reason and that necessity. For instance, if the Ugly Sisters are older than Cinderella, it is (in an iron and awful sense) *necessary* that Cinderella is younger than the Ugly Sisters. There is no getting out of it. Haeckel may talk as much fatalism about that fact as he pleases: it really must be. If Jack is the son of a miller, a miller is the father of Jack. Cold reason decrees it from her awful throne: and we in fairyland submit. If the three brothers all ride horses, there are six animals and eighteen legs involved: that is true rationalism, and fairyland is full of it.

But as I put my head over the hedge of the elves and began to take notice of the natural world, I observed an extraordinary thing. I observed that learned men in spectacles were talking of the actual things that happened – dawn and death and so on – as if *they* were rational and inevitable. They talked as if the fact that trees bear fruit were just as *necessary* as the fact that two and one trees make three. But it is not. There is an enormous difference by the test of fairyland; which is the test of the imagination. You cannot *imagine* two and one not making three. But you can easily imagine trees not growing fruit; you can imagine them growing golden candlesticks or tigers hanging on by the tail.

Now, it will be objected that *moral* truths do not fall into the same category as the mathematical or metaphysical certitudes Chesterton speaks of here. This is a mistake born of the modern habit of cultural relativism. One could *imagine* a world where the three brothers could all ride horses and have twenty-four legs involved instead of eighteen; all you need is a world where horses have six legs. But if you once grant that, you will discover that you are no longer talking about horses; you are talking about a different animal that has been (confusingly and deceptively) allowed to usurp the common name of *Equus ferus caballus.*

Likewise, perhaps you can imagine a species of creature for whom it is actually good that they should kill their friends or devour their young; but when you do so, you are no longer talking of *Homo sapiens* or any of his near relatives (real or hypothetical). The nature of the animal is so different that its lessons cannot be taken as applicable to us humans; the ethics of the Natural Anthropophagus are 'not addressed to our condition'. To pretend that they are is to tell a deep and awful lie. If you are going to draw lessons for human beings, you have to draw them from human life, or from something so closely analogous to it that the logic and the conclusions can be transferred back to humans.

The anthropomorphic animals of Aesop's fables are creatures of this kind, and indeed such beast-fables are prominent in the wisdom literature of many cultures. But the point would cease to apply if the animals stopped being anthropomorphic. We can readily perceive the lesson of the fox and the grapes, even though real foxes don't eat grapes, because real men and women do. We should be ill advised to draw a lesson from the female mantis, who (according to another kind of fable) consummates her nuptials by eating the bridegroom; because real men and women do *not* mate in that way. A woman who bit off her husband's head would find herself without a mate long before she reached the point of having children, and her amorous innovation would die out in the first generation. It would be contrary to the Customs.

The rule of fantasy is that the Customs remain the same; the stories may be about foxes or elves or creatures from Arcturus in the literal sense, but they must be applicable to human experience, and within the range of human sympathy, if they are to touch the reader's heart and not merely titillate her desire for novelty. To quote from *Orthodoxy* again:

> If you draw a giraffe, you must draw him with a long neck.
> If, in your bold creative way, you hold yourself free to draw a

giraffe with a short neck, you will really find that you are not free to draw a giraffe.

Human beings really do have a rather determinate nature. Our differences, spectacular as they may seem, are all founded upon a bedrock of similarity. Aristotle, in his *Nicomachean Ethics*, investigated these universals of human nature, and drew up a moral code based on them. C. S. Lewis, in *The Abolition of Man*, has shown how the same code, restated in but slightly different terms, recurs over and over in every cultural tradition on every continent. The kind of maxims that Lewis collected are another variety of wisdom literature, and a splendid real-life instance of the general consistency of 'the Customs' even in strictly human affairs. If, in your bold creative way, you draw a man without this bedrock ethical structure, you will really find that you are not free to draw a man.

The same stricture applies to that staple of fantasy, the Wise Old Man. Even if he is not technically a man, he has to say things that it would be wise for a man to say, or it will not appear as wisdom at all. Fantasy and near-fantasy books are filled with Wise Old Men, chiefly because Wise Old Men are useful figures to conduct maid-and-butler dialogues with Naive Young Heroes, but also, perhaps, because that canny old charlatan Jung listed the Wise Old Man prominently among his archetypes. The W.O.M. has become part of the furniture of Fantasyland, and the hacks at the Old Baloney Factory haven't got the guts or the imagination to do without him. Unfortunately, while these Wise Old Men may be very old indeed, most of them seem singularly lacking in wisdom.

This, while regrettable, is hardly surprising. Wisdom is not a quality much sought after nowadays. The word sounds uncomfortably elitist and anti-subjective. It will not do to say that one person is wiser than another, unless one is prepared to say that one belief may be right and another wrong; and that is just the sort of thing we have grown too mealy-mouthed to say. It is the culmination of our collective amnesia. For two centuries, Western civilization has been growing steadily more infatuated with ephemeral knowledge at the expense of enduring truth. Ancient folktales and traditional songs have been replaced by pop-culture references; philosophy has declined into ideology; and wisdom, as an object of desire, has largely been supplanted by technical know-how. The very word *wizard*, which originally meant 'wise person', has come back into vogue as a label for people with the technological skill to do impressively difficult things as if by magic. Our ancestors, if educated, learnt Latin and quoted the Book of Proverbs; we learn XML and Java and quote the 'Chicken Soup' books I mentioned earlier.

> They think that [God] works like the factories in Claptrap, inventing every day a new machine which supersedes the old. As machines are among the very few things that they do know something about, they cannot help thinking that everything is like them.

That is Lewis again, castigating the 'Anti-Romantics' in *The Pilgrim's Regress*. He could have aimed this barb at the Postmodernists if they had existed in his day, or the Moral Relativists, or any of the philosophically vacuous people who think human nature as changeable as popular opinion. Whatever else has changed in the last thousand years, the human animal has not changed, and neither has the human brain. We cannot invent a new emotion, any more than a new primary colour. Birth and death are with us yet, as mysterious and awful as they were to our Neolithic ancestors, and as shrouded in rituals and taboos. Marriage persists strongly, despite the best efforts of the sexual revolutionaries, and even religion has stubbornly falsified every prediction that it would disappear. Computers ten years ago ran Windows XP, and computers ten years hence may run Windows 10 or iOS 12 or Android Goody Gum Drops; but the operating system of the human soul has not changed in all our recorded history.

I am convinced that this largely accounts for our present hankering for fantasy. Fantasy worlds seldom seem to change much, and for the most part they do not change in technology at all. In Elfland men still fight each other with swords, or shoot arrows at one another, and they have never learnt to build machines more complicated than a simple water-powered grist-mill or sawmill. In other words, they live pretty much as humans lived from the invention of agriculture to the beginning of the Industrial Revolution. (Of course there was great change during that long span of time; but it usually occurred so slowly that a man could grow old and die in the same world and culture he was born in.) Fantasy is a zoo, as it were, where we can see humans in a clever imitation of their native habitat. Our own habitat changes so fast that it can hardly be called native to any of us. I was born in the 1960s, and already I often feel like an exile from a country that no longer exists. For a people almost wholly ignorant of history, fantasy serves as a useful palliative for culture shock. It gives us an ersatz feeling of continuity.

But it is only ersatz, for the most part, because it has no real connection to the common culture of preindustrial man. Nowhere is this easier to see than when an author tries to put words of wisdom in a character's mouth. Ursula Le Guin said, you will recall, that archaism is something you have got to learn how to do before you can do it. The same is true of wisdom. The collective experience and understanding of any preindustrial people can be found in its store of proverbs, adages, fables, folktales, ballads, poems, and nursery rhymes. There is more homely philosophy in a rhyme like 'Simple Simon' than in many a learned tract. As late as the 18th century, Benjamin Franklin seized upon aphorisms and gnomic verses as a way to inculcate strength of character among his American readers.

Some familiar examples of this kind of wisdom:

> Pride goeth before destruction, and an haughty spirit before a fall. —*Proverbs 16:18*
> Whatsoever a man soweth, that shall he also reap. —*St. Paul, Galatians 6:7*
> It is better to light a single candle than to curse the darkness. —*Confucius*
> A liar will not be believed, even when he speaks the truth. —*Aesop*

Early to bed and early to rise, Makes a man healthy, wealthy, and wise. —*Franklin, Poor Richard's Almanac*

If wishes were horses, beggars might ride. —*English proverb, as collected by John Ray*

There is a definite manner that all these have in common: pithy, sententious, unabashedly prescriptive. All are what is now called 'simplistic'; but this popular wisdom is far from simplistic, for often a culture will have two familiar adages that appear to contradict one another, warning against opposite extremes. Sometimes a single saying expresses both horns of the dilemma:

Answer not a fool according to his folly, lest thou also be like unto him. Answer a fool according to his folly, lest he be wise in his own conceit. —*Proverbs 26:4-5*

Now, there is an art to constructing adages, and it has largely been lost. A few modern writers, professionally familiar with the old documents, have managed to acquire the knack and use it to good effect:

Oft evil will shall evil mar.

Oft the unbidden guest proves the best company.

It needs but one foe to breed a war, not two; and those who have not swords can still die upon them.

See the bear in his own den before you judge of his conditions.

The first three of those are from Tolkien, the fourth from Lewis. It is no accident that the readiest examples come from the Inklings, Oxford dons steeped in classic and mediaeval traditions, with a Christian conservatism that assigned living value and significance to the old chestnuts they found there.

Stephen R. Donaldson, though learned primarily in modern literature, as a student of English and a child of missionaries has enough of the same background to work in a similar style when he chooses:

He who waits for the sword to fall upon his neck will surely lose his head.

But now, I am afraid, it is time for some counterexamples. Let us begin with this:

Perfect speed is being there.

That is from *Jonathan Livingston Seagull*, and well exemplifies the modern Western bumper-sticker koan, the paradox that seems profound but is really meaningless. Richard Bach's aphorism is certainly not true of physical velocity, which is what Jonathan is taught to apply it to; it leads not to instant apportation, the seagull's goal, but to standing still. To be everywhere at once may indeed be 'perfect speed', but this discovery leaves us, who can be in only one place at a time, no better off. Like that sweet romance in which the bride eats the head of the groom, it is not addressed to our condition.

A proverb should be plain and vivid, and the metaphor, if any, obvious; and the application in daily life should be clear. This one is vague and abstract, and can only be interpreted by supplying a metaphor to which the saying itself supplies no key. It is true that *Jonathan Livingston Seagull* as a whole supplies a kind of key; but not a useful one. The book is 'inspirational' without being wise, but written in language cribbed from pop philosophy, to lend it a spurious air of wisdom. Those who know best the philosophical traditions thus traduced are least forgiving of the result.

One of the worst, or at least most infamous, offenders is our old friend Terry Goodkind. The same sterility of imagination and ineptitude of style that characterize his work as a whole appear in concentrated form when he tries to offer words of wisdom. Here are a few of his 'Wizard's Rules':

People are stupid; given proper motivation, almost anyone will believe almost anything. Because people are stupid, they will believe a lie because they want to believe it's true, or because they are afraid it might be true.

The Wizard's Fourth Rule, he called it. He said that there was magic in sincere forgiveness, in the Fourth Rule. Magic to heal. In forgiveness you grant, and more so in the forgiveness you receive.

Life is the future, not the past.

Deserve Victory.

The last 'rule' listed above, by the way, was a slogan used in Britain during the Second World War to build civilian morale, and was conspicuously ineffective. The others run the gamut from New Age platitudes to expressions of boundless cynicism.

At one end of the scale, the 'magic' of forgiveness is a fine thing, but the Rule, for all its mock-poetic wind, says nothing about what that magic *does*. Compare William Blake's verse on a similar subject:

> I was angry with my friend:
> I told my wrath, my wrath did end.
> I was angry with my foe:
> I told it not, my wrath did grow.

That tells you something about the *effects* of forgiveness, instead of merely expelling gas about how magical it all is. There is no place for vague rhapsodizing in 'rules' or proverbs, which need to be pithy and precise. Nothing so unspecific and unmemorable would pass the tests of use and time; but then, Goodkind's world has such an exiguous past that perhaps the test of time has never been applied there.

At the opposite end, 'People are stupid' is a recipe for pride, an ill-founded feeling of superiority to one's fellow man, and the ready temptation to Machiavellian manipulation. In cynicism, but not in elegance of expression, it matches *Mundus vult decipi, ergo decipiatur.* James Branch

Cabell, himself an arch-cynic, made that the motto of his fictitious *pays* of Poictesme, and for good reason: he was mocking everything within reach, and the whole 'Biography of the Life of Manuel' constitutes a kind of *reductio ad absurdum* of human behaviour and ambition. Goodkind, on the other hand, would have us believe that he is serious.

Actually, all these Rules are written in an awkward and clunky style severely at odds with the laconic poetry of the traditional proverb. Even so recent a coinage as Murphy's Law has been trimmed to fit that standard. According to his son Robert, Major Murphy originally said something like this:

> If there's more than one way to do a job, and one of those ways
> will result in disaster, then somebody will do it that way.

But it was not in anything like that form that the phrase caught on. It had to be purified of its complexities and caveats, and cast in the strict mnemonic form of the popular adage, before it could take its place in the public mind. In the process, unfortunately, it lost much of its original meaning, and the wisdom of the original has turned to cynicism in the final form:

> If something can go wrong, it will.

It says less than the original, but says it better, which matters more: it is easy to remember and falls trippingly from the tongue. The original Law has been worn smooth in passing from hand to hand.

Goodkind's Rules have not been refined in this way, much to their detriment. By turns over-serious, self-important, cynical and empty, they have the heaviness of gold without the glitter. So does lead. We do not make crowns and sceptres out of lead; and the Golden Rule takes hold of the mind and heart as no leaden rule could ever do. If we are going to have imitations of ancient wisdom in our fiction, they had better be wise, and they had better be well expressed. Too many of Goodkind's are neither.

There is a koan to the effect that a wheel is useless unless it has a hole in the centre to revolve around. But the function of the hole is not to remain empty, but to attach the wheel to the axle. The 'wisdom' of authors like Goodkind reminds me of a wheel without an axle: it will roll, but it cannot carry the cart. Considering that his books are positively hagridden by his Message of watered-down Randism, it seems odd to accuse them of thematic vacuity; but the accusation holds just the same. As soon as he actually expresses the so-called wisdom that makes up the burden of the Message, any wary and experienced reader can see that it is really no wisdom at all, but something ginned up out of platitudes and errors.

Goodkind, alas, is far from the worst offender. Hundreds of his fellow authors have not even a vacuous message. These are the timid souls who merely tell us that their Wise Old Men are wise, without ever offering a sample of their wisdom. Their books are full of wizards in the merely technical sense, enormously powerful in magic, but equally weak in philosophy. Of course a wise man need not expound his philosophy in a nutshell to prove that he is wise; but in too many cases we cannot even infer from the context of his actions what his philosophy is. Belgarath, to return to one of my earlier whipping-boys, has no philosophy at all except 'The Prophecy is always right'. His companions are even more alarmingly vapid. And there are scores of characters like him in the genre, wise men who show no sign of wisdom.

Perhaps it is this, even more than the derivative nature of their plots and settings, that makes so many fantasy authors' books so unrewarding. Their heroes exert themselves mightily to save the world, but they have never even asked the questions whose answers might make a world worth saving.

WHY ARE DRAGONS
AFRAID OF AMERICANS?

The chief business of an essayist – I speak here of the kind of essayist that I occasionally manage to be, and that better men than I are sometimes reduced to when not at their best – is to tilt at windmills. The second greatest delight such an essayist can know is to tilt at a windmill, in the full knowledge and expectation that it *is* really a windmill, and that he shall end by making a quixotic fool of himself, and discover in the heat of combat that it is only a giant after all.

I say '*only* a giant' advisedly. A windmill is an awful thing, in more than one sense of the word: a soulless creature born of sheer inanimate nature, grinding without desire, crushing without intent, turning its tireless arms in response to a commandment more inexorable than the law of the Medes and Persians, which altereth not. I believe that the windmill was invented by Koshchei the Deathless, while wearing the guise in which he used to appear to James Branch Cabell – 'the Master of Things As They Are', as Cabell called him. How wonderful it is, then, having tried one's lance against a windmill, to find that after all it is just another creature of flesh and blood like oneself – bigger and stronger, no doubt, but just as fallible, just as uncertain, just as liable to err, to weary, and to die. The *greatest* delight of an essayist is to tilt at a windmill and find that it really *is* a windmill, that one has crossed lances, in some way, with the fundamental bedrock of reality. But that experience is a great deal rarer.

So I spend a lot of my time tilting at windmills, and most of them, as it turns out, are nothing but giants. This language is figurative. I mean that I pick quarrels with the conventional wisdom or fashionable opinion that different sorts of people are apt to accept as unalterable truth; and then I find that they are only opinions, and dubiously founded ones at that – or else I do not. Since *both* conventional wisdom and fashionable opinion are fallible and largely wrong, and nearly everybody takes comfort in one or the other, I make a terrible nuisance of myself to virtually everybody. In the past, for instance, I have gone jousting in aid of Ursula K. Le Guin, and particularly for her views on the diction and rhetoric of fantasy, though she needs my help almost as much as a whale needs a life jacket. Today I feel the urge to turn my lance against her, or against one of her windmills, and see whether I score a hit on a giant.

The occasion of this joust is the arrival today, per post, of a long-awaited copy of *The Language of the Night*, Ms. Le Guin's first, and perhaps best-known, book of critical essays. It has been allowed to go out of print, but several of the essays in it have been so widely reprinted that not even the folly of publishers has suppressed their well-earned fame. Some of these I first read long ago, when I was in my early youth, and Ms. Le Guin was already an accomplished past master of her craft; which is odd, because I am now several aeons older than the hills, and Ms. Le Guin is still only in her early eighties. I attribute this discrepancy to the well-known habit women have of telling lies about their age.

Now, in those days, in the first flush of youth, or at least in an epoch when I was still thrusting upwards by orogeny and not merely wearing down by erosion, I was strongly impressed, and somewhat flattered, by the first proper essay in *Language*, which bears the fine polemical title, 'Why Are Americans Afraid of Dragons?' Impressed, because I had not much experience of the world, and thought that the people who *seemed* in public not to care for fantasy or imaginative fiction must necessarily have the same fault in private life; flattered, because by implication I was one of the happy few not so afflicted. I was far from being the only one so impressed, or so flattered. This essay, or rather, the extraordinary claim made in its title, has been taken up into the received wisdom of Western culture: so that people feel themselves wise and learned for granting the antecedent, or rather, begging the question, and simply *assuming* that Americans *are* afraid of dragons.

In support of the idea, I admit, Ms. Le Guin tells a pretty tale, and she could probably get the average jury to convict. To summarize baldly: America, more than any other country, is the heir to the Puritan tradition, which values worldly things only according to their immediate usefulness, and utterly rejects magic and wonder as tools of the Devil. Even when Americans (and their unenlightened brethren in other industrialized nations) reject the idea of the Devil, they retain a vague and rootless distrust of the sort of things that were once considered the Devil's handiwork, such as *l'art pour l'art*, and aesthetic experience, and the free play of the imagination. American *men* in particular are subject to this disease; they are wholly consumed by the hateful materialistic philosophy of 'get on or get out', and have a practised disdain, ultimately phobic in nature, for any kind of art or literature that will not immediately help them get money for themselves. However, like all those who reject the overt manifestations of fantasy, the American Male lets the irrational in by the back door of superstition; so he will sometimes let himself read bestsellers, because bestsellers are good business, and some of their luck may rub off by a kind of sympathetic magic. He is, of course, never consciously aware of such a motive, but it is there just the same, and plain enough for a Le Guin to diagnose. For the rest he will stick to non-fiction, or else

> end up watching bloody detective thrillers on the television, or reading hack Westerns or sports stories, or going in for pornography.... That all these genres are sterile, hopelessly sterile, is a reassurance to him rather than a defect. If they were genuinely realistic, which is to say genuinely imagined and imaginative, he would be afraid of them. Fake realism is the escapist literature of our time. And probably the ultimate escapist reading

is that masterpiece of total unreality, the daily stock market report.

Now this is a masterpiece of character assassination, and all the more because the victim is entirely imaginary. The American Male of this depiction never existed: not in 1974, when Le Guin wrote this rant against him; not in 1900, when imaginative and (in the old-fashioned sense) 'romantic' literature were being ruthlessly squeezed out of the limelight and into the backwaters of American culture; not in 1830, when American literature was just beginning to take a shape of its own, after the fallow half-century that followed the cultural severance of the colonies from Europe. Americans, of course, and even American males, are as varied a group as any other nationality you might choose to name, and more varied than most. There are Americans with the solid commercial practicality of the Dutch, the quick-witted rationality of the French, the dreamy and intermittently dangerous sentimentality of the Germans – to say nothing of the peculiar cultural complexions of the island nations of Europe. And that is only to count the immigrants who formed part of the cultural matrix in the earliest years of the Union. It leaves out the Slavs, the Mediterranean peoples, the Asians, the Africans (who were present in those early years, but forcibly prevented from contributing to the culture till later). For that matter, it leaves out the American Indians: Hiawatha and Black Hawk are as much a part of American culture and American history as Captain John Smith and Andrew Jackson.

For all this variety, one can still draw a sort of composite picture of what we might call the culturally typical American; that is, of the cultural qualities that were thoroughly boiled down in the 'melting pot', and became the common property of the whole nation. Our composite American has never shied away from fantasy or the imagination. He loved tall tales long before he learnt to read; and since he grew up in a landscape of wild and wonderful possibilities, he did not much care whether the tall tales were strictly impossible or not. He is equally delighted with Paul Bunyan and Johnny Appleseed. He will swallow the feats of Natty Bumppo, which are flatly impossible without being magical, right along with the ghost stories of Edgar Allan Poe, which are magical and might not be quite impossible.

He has the advantage of loving adventure stories, and the greater advantage of living in a land where adventure has never been banished 'beyond the fields we know' into the realms of fantasy. He likes to play at being a juvenile Don Quixote, like Tom Sawyer, or a juvenile Marco Polo, like Huckleberry Finn. He doesn't believe in dragons – quite – but he has cousins who went West by covered waggon and turned back because they 'saw the elephant'. He likes taking day trips into the future, conducted by the folks at the circus of science fiction, even though he knows that one day the voyage will be as permanent and estranging as Rip Van Winkle's. He enjoys travelling abroad, where he entertains himself by pretending to be a barbarian to scandalize the snobs; he had great fun playing this game in King Arthur's court.

His chief official hero is George Washington, a real person credited with doing things that never happened, like chopping down the celebrated cherry tree. His *unofficial* heroes include Bugs Bunny and Donald Duck, entirely unreal persons who somehow managed to accomplish all sorts of perfectly real things. American adventure fiction takes reality and fantasy, magic and technology, sober exploration and wild travellers' yarns, chucks them all up together in the air as high as they will go, and makes a glorious game of taking them just as they fall. It may happen to exclude the elements of fantasy in particular instances, but it has no prejudice against them; and neither, we must conclude, has its audience.

This is the common or melting-pot American, in the particularly masculine form that Ms. Le Guin has singled out for castigation: and if he is afraid of dragons at all, he is probably afraid that they may be a shade too dull for him. Old-world etiquette requires him to be a St. George and kill them, but he would really rather climb on their backs, rodeo style, and see if he can stay on for the whole eight seconds. He used to be wonderfully served by what we may call his *official* culture, the Arts and Literature and Other Good Things with Capital Letters. Cooper, Irving, Poe, Melville, Twain, O. Henry – the earlier part of American literary history is a glorious constellation of tall-tale tellers who didn't care a rap whether they were being 'realistic' or not. *Moby-Dick* is filled with painstaking detail about life aboard a whaling boat, but it is also the ultimate fish story about 'the one that got away'; the great white whale is as mythic a figure as the fish that swallowed Jonah, and the one has sometimes been mistaken for the other. The same whale (I have it on good authority) used to go by the name of Fastitocalon, and lurk about in the mediaeval bestiaries, pretending to be an island until unwary sailors tried to land on him and pitch a camp. Fantasy and realism play together with perfect freedom, *en tutoyant,* neither of them putting on airs or pretending to dominate the other.

It is sadly true, however, that the typical American, especially the *male* American, of the 1970s and thereabouts, as Ms. Le Guin knew him, did not have much time for fiction, except for the dull mass-produced stuff served to him by network television; and this phenomenon has got to be accounted for. He may not have been afraid of dragons, but there were certainly no dragons in his life. How can we account for this? The hypothesis suggests itself that it was the dragons who were afraid of the Americans, and not the other way round. Something *frightened them off.*

In 'On Fairy-Stories', J. R. R. Tolkien remarks that fantasy came to be associated with children, not because it was peculiarly suitable for them, but because their elders had ceased to like it; just as the old furniture in a house would be banished to the nursery for the children's use. But it was not only fantasy that was treated in this way. The whole tradition of adventure fiction – all the tropes and categories that descended ultimately from the mediaeval romance, and that were still called 'romantic' in English until that word was misappropriated and applied exclusively to love-stories – was quite abruptly banished from polite circles in the latter part of the nineteenth century, not only in the U.S. but in other industrial countries as well, and remained in exile until it crept back in through the new medium of the mass-market paperback in the years after the Second World War. If you want to examine the truth of this claim, you have only to consider the kinds of fiction that were regarded as 'boys' stories' in the first half of the twentieth century. This is George Orwell in 'Boys' Weeklies':

> Examination of a large number of these papers shows that, putting aside school stories, the favourite subjects are Wild West, Frozen North, Foreign Legion, crime (always from the detective's angle), the Great War (Air Force or Secret Service, not the infantry), the Tarzan motif in varying forms, professional football, tropical exploration, historical romance (Robin Hood, Cavaliers and Round-heads, etc.) and scientific invention. The Wild West still leads, at any rate as a setting, though the Red Indian seems to be fading out. The one theme that is really new is the scientific one. Death-rays, Martians, invisible men, robots, helicopters and interplanetary rockets figure largely: here and there there are even far-off rumours of psychotherapy and ductless glands.

Orwell is talking here about the British boys' magazines, but the same subjects, with minor variations, predominated in the American pulp magazines. The pulps showed far greater specialization than the British boys' weeklies; there were hundreds of titles, most of them monthly, against the ten papers that served the same market in the tight oligopoly of the British press; but then the American market was a bigger one, and it could be profitable to cater to quite small segments of it. Millions of Americans read the pulps for pleasure, and by no means all of them were boys; but the pulps were aimed at boys, edited for the reading-level of boys, and censored ferociously to keep out any subjects that might be thought to corrupt the impressionable minds of boys. It is this accident, by the way, that accounts for the remarkable sexlessness of 'Golden Age' science fiction.

Clearly there was an insatiable market for imaginative fiction; clearly our 'common American' had not died out, or given up reading, or even altered his tastes. But his preferred reading-matter had been banished to the cheapest magazines; the *literati* sneered and called it trash. After the pulp magazines disappeared, their place as the lowest common denominator of narrative fiction was taken over by television: very inadequately, for where there had been hundreds of pulps publishing thousands of stories per month, there were only three major television networks, broadcasting no more than about eighty prime-time series at any given time. There was much less variety in the televised pulp fiction of 1960 than in the printed pulp fiction of 1940. Naturally, the *literati* sneered at television twice as hard, fearing its tremendous reach and influence (and profitability) even more than they hated its deadly sameness.

But our common American stuck to his TV set and gave up, for the most part, even pretending to read 'serious' fiction, though he retained a certain taste for paperback Westerns and detective stories. The *literati* had not changed his tastes; they only managed to drive him out. They did not drive out his female counterpart, who was more interested in love-stories and domestic melodrama (which the electronic media call 'soap opera'). They could not; they needed her money. In the years after the Second World War, more than ever before, American popular fiction became a women's preserve. Those were the years that saw the rise of the Harlequin romance, and the mini-novel, 'complete in this issue', that was for a while a staple of the women's magazines; but also the rise of 'women's fiction', the ordinary bestselling novel that contained nothing *imaginative* in the wider sense, but pushed the emotional buttons of the average female reader within a carefully limited domain of 'realistic' domesticity.

Ms. Le Guin, of course, has no more time for this stuff than she has for the television shows that the menfolk were using to pass the time:

> [L]acking training and encouragement, her fancy is likely to glom on to very sickly fodder, such things as soap operas, and 'true romances', and nursy novels, and historico-sentimental novels, and all the rest of the baloney ground out to replace genuine imaginative works by the artistic sweatshops of a society that is profoundly distrustful of the uses of the imagination.

But once again, it does not occur to her that the Common American (Female Division) simply took the 'fodder' that was actually *available.*

The decision to push this kind of material was made from on high, in the élitist (and profoundly sexist) confines of the Higher Publishing. During what Ms. Le Guin herself has called the fifty-year halt of American feminism, women readers were not encouraged to read 'serious' fiction; but their interest in domestic matters and family drama (as old, and as evident, as the village gossip that has been with us since Neolithic times) meant that *some* of their interests could be catered to without risking the deep forbidden waters of the old-style romance. In these latter days, when women are perfectly free to range over the literary landscape however they choose, I have known any number of female readers who liked *both* 'sickly fodder' and 'genuine imaginative works' – women who voluntarily read (for example) 'nursy novels' in one mood, and science fiction in another, and find entertainment, even nourishment, in both. The readership of fantasy in the U.S. nowadays, I am told, is about three-fourths female. The same range of tastes, we may well suppose, was *latently* there in the women of fifty years ago; but the publishing business made a deliberate choice to cater to only one small part of that range.

It begins to look as if we are faced with a deliberate plot; and already I can hear a chorus warming up in the wings, getting ready to call me a crackpot and a conspiracy theorist. I can only reply that there *was* such a plot, and that some of the original principals have confessed. In *An Experiment in Criticism*, C. S. Lewis professed that he had never heard anyone actually and explicitly say that works of pure imagination (such as fantasy) were *per se* not literature, or *ought* not to be read; but I have seen both those claims made. As late as the early 1990s, I could go into any 'independent' bookshop in my home town and confidently expect *not* to find any science fiction or fantasy, except for stuff like *Nineteen Eighty-four* or *Lord of the Flies,* which had been suitably disinfected by being taught as Literature – so much the better if it was unbearably depressing, as those two books are to most people. If I wanted such books, I had to look in the chain bookshops, where the staff and the distant owners were not too proud to carry 'cheap commercial trash'.

But where did this attitude start? I have elsewhere repeated Dave Wolverton's assertion, which he can back with formidable evidence (as befits a retired professor), that it began with the American Socialist movement that arose around 1870, and in particular with William Dean Howells, the 'father of American realism'. Here it is again, from 'On Writing as a Fantasist':

> He claimed that authors had gone astray by being imitators of one another rather than of nature. He proscribed writing about 'interesting' characters – such as famous historical figures or creatures of myth. He decried exotic settings – places such as Rome or Pompeii, and he denounced tales that told of uncommon events. He praised stories that dealt with the everyday, where 'nobody murders or debauches anybody else; there is no arson or pillage of any sort; there is no ghost, or a ravening beast, or a hair-breadth escape, or a shipwreck, or a monster of self-sacrifice, or a lady five thousand years old in the course of the whole story'. He denounced tales with sexual innuendo. He said that instead he wanted to publish stories about the plight of the 'common man', just living an ordinary existence. Because Howells was the editor of the largest and most powerful magazine of the time (and because of its fabulous payment rates, a short story sale to that magazine could support a writer for a year or two), his views had a tremendous influence on American writers.

Howells was still alive, and still wielding that tremendous influence, in the first years of the twentieth century, when names like Henry James and Edith Wharton were the new giants of American letters. Howells's disciples – it is not too strong a word – had risen to the highest positions in New York publishing, and the editorships of the most prestigious literary reviews. Together they founded what we might call the 'secular Puritan' school of fiction, dominated by the idea that strict realism is the only valid form of literature, because only strict realism is *good* for you. And how do you know that it is good for you? Why, because it is *dull*. There are those who profess to be fascinated by James's and Wharton's fiction, but they are well outnumbered, as I believe, by those who admire their technique, but admit that the bulk of their stories, considered as stories, are terribly and sustainedly boring. This attitude of studied admiration for deliberate dulness was appallingly common at the time; it is brilliantly lampooned in Saki's short story, 'Filboid Studge', in which the world's worst breakfast cereal becomes a daily staple precisely because anything that foul-tasting *must* be good for you – if not nutritionally, then morally.

It was not only the younger writers who geared up to write literary Filboid Studge. Mark Twain's last years furnish sad evidence of Howells's power. Twain and Howells were close friends in those years, and Howells influenced Twain's work, I believe, markedly for the worse. Among my books are two volumes of Twain from the Library of America: one containing a sample of his shorter pieces from 1852 to 1890, the other from 1890 to his death in 1910. They might almost have been written by two different men. The stories in the first volume are imaginative, wild, free, and nearly always funny, in the finest tradition of the American tall tale. Those in the second volume are increasingly solemn, sober, preachy, and depressing, and when they depart from strict realism, it is apt to be in the service of heavy-handed satire, like the attack on religion in *The Mysterious Stranger*. Among these latter pieces is a little screed that he wrote to glorify Howells. In this, he makes a great effort to convince us that a little word-picture by Howells (of menial labourers shovelling snow in the Piazza San Marco in Venice) is a masterpiece of poetic prose. It isn't; it is a string of pretty words, prettily put together, and wasted on an utterly trivial object.

But Howells would not have it any other way; he devoutly believed literature *ought* to be about trivial objects. He thought that snow-shovellers in Venice were worth writing about precisely because they were ordinary and prosaic, and because they were poor and downtrodden; and if only the art of literature could be engaged to make them *seem* fascinating and important, it would enlist the sympathies of the middle classes on their behalf, and then – hey presto! The Socialist Utopia would ensue. This method was followed by Upton Sinclair and others, and ultimately perfected by Steinbeck. One could call it 'Socialist Realism for the bourgeoisie'. Such work has a powerful attraction for the *literati* to this day, for the *literati* are still Socialists for the most part, and are still, after all these years, waiting for their Utopia. The 'sentence cult', the habit of heaping extravagant praise upon works that combine exquisite prose with utterly vapid subject-matter, is as congenial to their ideology now as it was in Howells's time.

For it is the characteristic mark of the Utopian Socialist in particular (there are other and better kinds of Socialists) that he must be in a perpetual stew lest people hanker after the *wrong* Utopia. Even to find a modicum of happiness in this life is liable to be condemned by such people as 'escapism'; and of course stories of fantasy and adventure are 'escapist' by definition. It does not much matter whether the stories are realistic or not, in the sense of being formally possible in real life. The Utopian view is that 'realism' requires an unrelenting focus on the dreary, the depressing, the degrading; that, as Lenin put it, the worse things are, the better they are – for it is miserable people who can be talked into backing revolutions. Happy and contented people are too liable to accept the *status quo*.

The idea was perfectly expressed, back in the 1920s, by an American union organizer who complained because workingmen were buying motorcars:

> The Ford car has done an awful lot of harm to the unions
> here and everywhere else. As long as men have enough money
> to buy a second-hand Ford and tires and gasoline, they'll be out
> on the road and paying no attention to union meetings.

This kind of thinking – 'the worse, the better' – persisted strongly in Socialist parties all over the world until the 1980s, and in some of them it persists to this day. A genuine turning-point came in 1987, when another union leader – a British one, this time, the late Ron Todd – confessed that this whole method was mistaken:

> What do you say to a docker who earns £400 a week, owns his house, a new car, a microwave and a video, as well as a small place near Marbella? You do not say, 'Let me take you out of your misery, brother.'

But misery remains a selling-point for the *literati;* as long as it is other people's misery. The élite of the New York publishing business, and the élite of the famous reviews, all earned their élitehood by acquiring the strongest possible taste for Filboid Studge; they cannot possibly admit that the game is up, that the unwashed masses were right all along to take their nourishment from food that tasted good. It was these élites that fought to keep J. K. Rowling off the *Times* bestseller list (and succeeded in banishing her to a separate children's list); it was their British counterparts who cried out that literature was dead because polls of the British reading public showed that *The Lord of the Rings* was regarded as the greatest novel of the twentieth century. According to the Filboid Studge theory, no work of fantasy ('escapist trash') should have been allowed on the list at all; the highest place should have been reserved for *Ulysses,* no matter how the vote had to be rigged to make it come out right.

Tom Shippey tells a lovely tale about a famous British critic who said, on hearing that *The Lord of the Rings* had topped the poll: 'Has it? Oh dear, oh dear, oh dear.' Such things are not supposed to happen; and to a good Utopian Socialist, who still believes in the Marxist dogmas he imbibed in his credulous youth, such things *cannot* happen. History is the inevitable progress of humanity out of the ignorant past and into the glorious Marxist future. Fantasy is dead, the adventure story is dead, just as religion and *laissez-faire* are supposed to be dead; our glorious predecessors killed them a hundred years ago. If the dead are seen walking abroad, they can only be ghosts; and we cannot believe in ghosts. For a Utopian of 2000, the continued popularity of Tolkien was intolerable, as the victories of Thatcher and Reagan were for a Utopian of 1980. They refuted the theories; they confounded the prophecies.

In 1974, when Ms. Le Guin wrote her snide attack on the taste of the American public, it was still just barely possible to believe that the Socialist Utopia was still inevitable; and rather easier to believe that the triumph of literary realism was complete. At that time, the publishing industry had convinced itself that fantasy was unsalable after all, that Tolkien had been a passing fad of the hippie culture, like tie-dye or acid rock. But it was only the publishers who believed it. The American public were never deceived. Many of them had never heard of Tolkien, or of any modern fantasy for grown-ups; the knowledge had been carefully kept from them. But the attitude that Le Guin fathers onto them, the *contempt* for fantasy and adventure fiction, hardly existed outside the circle of the literary élite and their hangers-on.

Some people – it was a common thing in academia – hated fantasy because it was fashionable to hate it, because that was the way to get up and get on in their profession. Some had an honest distaste for it. Some people loved it. The great mass of the people *liked* fantasy, when they could get it; they enjoyed taking their children to Disney movies (often more than the children themselves did). TV programs like *Bewitched* were always popular. As fantasy goes, these things were pretty thin gruel; but a man will take thin gruel and be glad of it, if he can get no other food. But it was never true that the mass of the American people were *afraid* of fantasy, or of imaginative fiction in general.

Just three years after Ms. Le Guin published 'Why Are Americans Afraid of Dragons?', the dam burst once and for all. In one amazing year, 1977, the film industry was changed for ever by the astounding success of a fantasy movie with science-fiction visuals – *Star Wars.* The biggest selling book of the year was *The Silmarillion.* In the same year, *The Sword of Shannara* and *The Chronicles of Thomas Covenant the Unbeliever* proved that Tolkien was not alone, that there was a huge pent-up demand for fantasy by other authors as well. By the early eighties, science fiction and fantasy books were frequent bestsellers, and SF and fantasy movies were reliable box-office hits. The Common American (of both sexes) was back; the American tall tale, in all its forms, was alive and impossibly well. *Raiders of the Lost Ark* showed that the pure adventure story, even without the trimmings of SF, had lost none of its old power to enchant an audience. The *auteurs* of the 1970s 'new cinema' have been mourning their lost glory and counting their losses ever since. They tried to conquer Hollywood for the kingdom of Filboid Studge – and failed. And since that day, the very citadel of Filboid Studge in America, the New York Literary Establishment, has been under siege.

That, in brief, is the story of the American who was never afraid of dragons. He took to dragons with childlike delight, as soon as the dragons were allowed to get near him again. And sad to say, the people who were afraid of dragons all along – the people who went to war upon the dragons, and made the dragons afraid of *them* – were not the hated capitalists, the money men reading 'that masterpiece of total unreality, the daily stock market report'. They were the *literati* themselves, the Progressives, the enlightened and cultured ones – people a lot more like Ms. Le Guin than the straw men she mistook for her opponents. Like Pogo in the famous comic strip (another masterpiece of the American imagination), Ms. Le Guin could aptly have proclaimed: 'We have met the enemy, and he is us.'

CREATIVE DISCOMFORT AND *STAR WARS*

The fact is that this script feels rushed and not thought out,
probably because it was rushed and not thought out.
> —*'Harry S. Plinkett' (Mike Stoklasa)*

They're already building sets. God help me! I'm going to have
to start this script pretty soon.
> —*George Lucas*

It is not actually true that 'all good writing is rewriting'. It would be nearer the truth to say that all good *ideas* are second ideas – or third, fourth, or 157th ideas. Writers are notoriously divisible into two warring camps, 'outliners' and 'pantsers'. One of the most common triggers for a rewrite happens when you come up with a brilliant new idea halfway through a draft – and that idea makes a hash of everything you have already written. This, in the war of the writers, is a powerful weapon against the pantsers.

Jeff Bollow, for instance, in his book *Writing FAST,* recommends that you get your ideas right *first,* and write the draft later; but he also tells you never to use the first idea that comes to mind, for that only trains your mind to be lazy. If you do your brainstorming properly, and don't start actually *writing* until your ideas are solid, you are much less likely to have to tear up a draft and start over. John Cleese touched on the same point in his 1991 talk on creativity:

> Before you take a decision, you should always ask yourself the question, 'When does this decision have to be taken?' And having answered that, you defer the decision until then, in order to give yourself maximum pondering time, which will lead you to the most creative solution.
>
> And if, while you're pondering, somebody accuses you of indecision, say: 'Look, babycakes, I don't have to decide till Tuesday, and I'm not chickening out of my creative discomfort by taking a snap decision before then. That's too easy.'

That creative discomfort can make all the difference between great writing and dreck. One could argue the point endlessly, for there are examples to the contrary – snap decisions that turned out to be brilliant, slowly gestated ideas that still turned out useless. I would maintain that such cases are outliers: so much depends on the talent of the individual writer, and on sheer luck. What we want here is a controlled experiment. We could learn a great deal by taking the same writer and putting him through a series of similar projects. In half of them, he would have all the time he wanted to brainstorm, to throw away ideas when he came up with better ones, to tear up drafts, to indulge his creative discomfort. In the other half, whenever he had to make a decision, he would simply take the first workable idea that came to mind. Unfortunately, we can't hire a writer to go through such an experiment. Fortunately, the experiment has already been made. The writer's name was George Lucas.

Michael Kaminski's *Secret History of Star Wars* (both the book and the website) describes the experiment and its results in fascinating detail. For my present purpose, however, I will take only a few points from Kaminski's (and Lucas's) work, specifically about the writing process: two from the 'Original Trilogy', and three from the prequels. To begin, then:

In the early 1970s, fresh off the unexpected success of *American Graffiti*, Lucas decided to try his hand at a rollicking space opera in the style of the old *Flash Gordon* serials. Thwarted in his attempt to buy the film rights to *Flash Gordon* itself, he began scribbling names and ideas on notepads, trying to come up with a space opera all of his own. He read and reread pulp science fiction stories obsessively, especially E. E. 'Doc' Smith's Lensman books. After a million and three false starts (this number has been verified by Science), he sent his agent a very brief synopsis called *The Journal of the Whills*, which began with the following helpful sentence:

> This is the story of Mace Windy, a revered Jedi-Bendu of Opuchi, as related to us by C. J. Thorpe, padawaan learner to the famed Jedi.

The agent, Jeff Berg, reacted approximately as follows: 'Mace Who, a revered What of Where, as related by the Whatsit learner to the famed How's That Again? You gotta be kidding me!' He gently advised his client to rewrite the synopsis in English.

This was not an easy request for the young Lucas to fulfil. From beginning to end, the *Star Wars* saga – as it would eventually be called – is filled with characters who speak no English at all. But he did *approximately* comply, and eventually came up with a treatment for a project called (at this point) *The Star Wars*. He lifted most of the story from Kurosawa's *Hidden Fortress*. As in the Kurosawa film, the lead characters are a general and a princess, who are trying to escape the clutches of a wicked and decadent empire during a period of civil war. The general's name is Luke Skywalker.

It took four years to turn this sketchy treatment into a movie. Along the way, Lucas put the script through four full drafts and innumerable small revisions. Seldom has a script been so struggled over. In some versions, the hero's name is not Skywalker but Starkiller. (Sometimes both names, confusingly, are used in the same draft for two different characters.) The Jedi were written out of the second draft entirely, and then put back into the third. 'The Force' (sometimes called 'the Force of Others') is sometimes a purely mental power, somewhat similar to hypnosis, sometimes a physical super-power accessible to a trained mind. Han Solo was conceived as a repulsive green alien; then the green alien was renamed Greedo, and Han Solo (now a human) killed him.

Lucas, in those days, had a well-justified lack of confidence in his writing skills. Fortunately, he had continual recourse to help from better qualified people – Gary Kurtz, Francis Ford Coppola, and his wife Marcia, among many others. Important bits of the script were reworked on the set by the actors. Harrison Ford famously told Lucas: 'George, you can type this shit, but you can't say it' – and then turned it into something that he *could* say. Lucas borrowed lines and motifs wherever he could, and when he could not borrow, he stole; but he remained in control at all times, and gradually shaped this magpie's collection of material into a classic fairy tale – a fairy tale in space.

The original *Star Wars* became the surprise blockbuster of 1977, the biggest pop-culture phenomenon since Beatlemania. (I first saw it, as a boy of ten, at the old North Hill cinema in Calgary. In addition to the title, the marquee carried a shameless political plug: 'R2-D2 FOR MAYOR.') Lucas's share of the profits was enough to bankroll a sequel without any financial input from a studio. Writing and directing the first film had nearly killed him; this time he hired help. The sequel was directed by Irvin Kershner, who would leave his own imprint on the story; but we are concerned here with the script. For that, Lucas wanted an honest-to-goodness, old-school space opera writer. A friend suggested Leigh Brackett: 'Here is someone who wrote the cantina scene in *Star Wars* better than you did.' Kaminski describes what happened next:

> [Lucas] contacted the elderly Brackett, who was living in Los Angeles at that time, and asked her to write *Star Wars II*. 'Have you ever written for the movies?' Lucas asked her.
>
> 'Yes, I have,' Brackett replied simply – she began recounting her credits, which included *Rio Bravo, El Dorado* and *The Big Sleep,* co-written with William Faulkner, the Nobel-prize-winning novelist.

An awkward silence followed. 'Are you *that* Leigh Brackett?' Lucas gasped.

'Yes,' she replied. 'Isn't that why you called me in?'

'No,' Lucas said, 'I called you in because you were a pulp science fiction writer.'

The Empire Strikes Back took less reworking than the original *Star Wars*. Partly this was because most of the principal characters had already been established, and much of the world-building was already worked out. Also, Leigh Brackett was simply a much more accomplished writer than Lucas. Unfortunately, she died shortly after completing the first draft, and Lucas was once more thrown upon his own resources. He did a very rough second draft – more like a treatment based on Brackett's first draft, incorporating some of the changes he wanted to make – before turning the job over to Lawrence Kasdan, whose work on *Raiders of the Lost Ark* had thoroughly impressed him.

The general sequence of the script remained much the same in each version, starting with the rebels on the ice planet, then splitting up the cast as Luke went for his Jedi training, and ending with the climactic encounter with Darth Vader. The love story between Han and Leia was developed – here, again, Lucas stole what he could not borrow – with dialogue lifted from, of all places, *Gone With the Wind*. Here is a bit of dialogue from the book, between Rhett Butler and Scarlett O'Hara:

> 'I'll bet you a box of bonbons against—' His dark eyes wandered to her lips. 'Against a kiss.'
>
> 'I don't care for such personal conversation,' she said coolly and managed a frown. 'Besides, I'd just as soon kiss a pig.'
>
> 'There's no accounting for tastes and I've always heard the Irish were partial to pigs – kept them under their beds, in fact. But, Scarlett, you need kissing badly.'

A good thief steals without getting caught; a great thief doesn't care whether he is caught, for he makes the stolen goods his own. Somewhere along the way, someone – Lucas, Brackett, Kasdan, or Kershner – came up with a change that turned this rather arch dialogue into a defining moment for the characters and a classic scene in cinema:

> **Han Solo:** Afraid I was gonna leave without giving you a good-bye kiss?
> **Princess Leia:** I'd just as soon kiss a Wookiee.
> **Han Solo:** I can arrange that. You could use a good kiss.

This was all very well; and between Kasdan's snappy dialogue and Kershner's mastery of emotional range as a director, the Han–Leia element of the story blossomed spontaneously. But that was only a subplot. A terrible shadow hung over the main plot: the shadow of Luke's father.

Father Skywalker had actually appeared in one draft of the original *Star Wars* script, before Lucas decided that he was already dead when the story began. Now he somehow had to be worked into the sequel. One could hardly film a dramatic scene about a man who had been dead for twenty years. That meant that the other characters had to *talk* about him. 'Show, don't tell' is a much abused bit of advice, but in drama and film, it really does apply. Showing saves time, and uses the full visual effect of the medium to convey an emotional impact that mere talking can never match. The conflict between the good Jedi, represented by Father Skywalker, and the evil Sith, represented by Darth Vader, could not easily be *shown*. The only way was to bring in Father Skywalker's ghost along with Obi-Wan's, as Leigh Brackett did in her first draft; and that, clearly, was one ghost too many.

Unless—

Inspiration struck.

Unless Father Skywalker and Darth Vader were the same person.

It was a brilliant idea: simple, dramatic, crackling with emotional force. It simplified the story, got rid of the extra ghost, and gave the whole script a powerful new unity. Before the change, Luke was separated from Han and Leia, not just physically, but thematically. He was going off to Dagobah to follow in his father's footsteps; Han and Leia were fleeing to

Bespin to escape from Vader's fleet. But if Luke's father *was* Vader, that tied their motives together and welded the plot into a single, consistent emotional arc.

This is the kind of idea that is worth tearing up a draft for. From the original *Journal of the Whills,* it took Lucas five years to come up with it. Fortunately, this change did not require any changes to the first film – though it made Obi-Wan a liar, a fact for which his ghost would offer a lame excuse in *Return of the Jedi.* (He would have done better to admit that he was afraid to tell Luke too much of the truth.) It turned the second film into a *tour de force.* And it set up the conditions and the conflicts for the third film. What's more, it did not require any significant change to the scene-by-scene structure of Leigh Brackett's first draft; it only gave the scenes a new and deeper meaning. Unlike the four major drafts of *Star Wars,* which changed the original story beyond recognition, the redrafts of *Empire* only added strength to a structure that was already sound.

When it became clear that *Star Wars* was a hit, and sequels would be called for, Lucas gave out that it was the first episode in a twelve-part series that he called 'The Adventures of Luke Skywalker'. In 1979, this idea disappeared down the memory hole. The first film became Episode IV, with the subtitle 'A New Hope' – which was added to the opening crawl for the theatrical re-release in 1981. *Star Wars* became the overall series title – a sound commercial decision, given the immense value of the brand name Lucas had created. The number of films in the projected series was cut down to nine. In a particularly Orwellian move, Lucas published the 'official' screenplay of *Star Wars* in 1979, labelled 'Episode IV: A New Hope', and incorporating many changes made between the fourth draft and the final movie; but he let on that this was the actual fourth draft, as written in 1976. It was the first of many attempts he would make to rewrite his own history. 'Greedo shot first' has a long lineage, if not an honourable one.

The Empire Strikes Back, as it turned out, was a brilliant movie; the trouble was that Lucas didn't want brilliance, didn't particularly understand it, and had not much idea how to make use of it. All along, he had wanted *Empire* to be short, quick-moving, and upbeat, like its predecessor; he was unhappy that Kasdan and Kershner turned it into something slower and grander and more introspective, and furiously angry with Kurtz for letting them go far over budget to do it. The immediate upshot was that Kurtz was replaced: Howard Kazanjian was hired to produce *Return of the Jedi*, in the hope that he would prove more obedient.

Jedi begins the downward spiral of the *Star Wars* sequels. Already we begin to see Lucas losing patience with his creative discomfort, taking snap decisions, seeking the easy way out of plot difficulties. He had already had the idea that Luke would have a sister, another potential Jedi; she appears under the name of Nellith in Brackett's draft. That, and Yoda's cryptic statement in *Empire*, 'There is another,' seem originally to have been intended as setup for Episodes VII through IX – and to heighten the immediate tension, by suggesting that Luke himself was expendable after all, and might not survive. But by the time he began work on *Jedi*, he was growing sick of the whole *Star Wars* phenomenon; he no longer had any intention of making six more episodes. So he took the easy way out by making Leia Luke's sister, and also the 'other' that Yoda spoke of. There was nothing in Leia's character to suggest a potential Jedi; but she was already *there*, and indeed, the only significant female character in the series. It was simply easier to write her as the 'other' than to introduce a new character for the purpose.

However, *Jedi* still works reasonably well. It carries on with the momentum generated by *Empire*, somewhat diminished by disco dance numbers and burp jokes, and by the need to find screen time for far too many Ewoks. Kershner and Kurtz were gone, but Kasdan was still on board as co-writer, and he outdid himself in developing the final three-way confrontation between Luke, Vader, and the Emperor. Lucas's snap decisions, at this stage, were all about tying up loose ends of subplots; they could not detract from the main story of the film.

Let us skip forward a bit.

Fifteen years later, Lucas was hard at work on Episode I, to which he gave the puzzling title, *The Phantom Menace*. This time, he was the sole (credited) screenwriter, as well as the director, executive producer, chief cook, bottle-washer, studio mogul, greenlighter, Howard Hughes, and Citizen Kane. Unlike *Empire* and *Jedi,* the new script was his baby, solely – and he had not improved as a screenwriter with the years. When Kasdan was brought in to rewrite the second draft of *Empire,* he was incredulous at the sheer badness of the dialogue; he had not heard the inside story about all of Lucas's helpers on the original *Star Wars* script. This time, Lucas's inadequacies would be exposed to the world's naked and unforgiving gaze.

I will pass over the inadequacies of the dialogue in the prequels, except to point out that with a very little more creative discomfort, Lucas could have hired a script doctor – a younger equivalent of Kasdan – to go over the lines and make them read more naturally. Lucas's dialogue is too literal, too 'on the nose': he never learnt the discipline of trusting his actors to *act.* Things that could be better conveyed by indirection – an elliptical remark, delivered with the right tone and facial expressions – were stated baldly, in terms that left the actors very little to do. Partly, as I have heard, this was done to make the script easier to translate into foreign languages, in which the subtleties of the original might be lost. If that is so, it would have done no harm to save Lucas's version as a master script for translators, and then hire a script doctor to translate it *into English,* inserting subtleties as required. But nobody seems to have thought of doing this.

What made *Phantom* so disappointing to grownups, and especially to those with fond memories of the characters and lines from *Empire* and *Jedi,* was that apart from the brilliant CGI work, it seemed to be built out of Tinkertoys. Every character and every action were obviously designed to get from one plot point to the next with a minimum of creative effort, and most of the plot points were apparently designed to lead into the visual set-pieces – the pod race, the battle on Naboo, and the utterly ridiculous scene in which the nine-year-old Anakin blows up the droid control ship with a one-man fighter that *he doesn't even know how to fly.*

The cumulative effect is bizarre: you might say that the picture had the brush-strokes of a Turner landscape, but the composition of a connect-the-dots puzzle.

Lucas did not write the *Phantom* script quickly; but he had many other cares, thanks to the multitude of hats he was wearing, and the script shows abundant signs that he skimped on the work. I will take one case as a sufficient example: the dire origin story of C-3PO.

Let us begin with the obvious. Young Anakin claims that he built Threepio to help his mother around the house. His mother, mind you, is a *slave:* she is supposed to *be* the help, not *receive* the help. This raises an awkward question. Droids are the accepted substitute for slave labour in the *Star Wars* universe. Why, then, does a scrap dealer, with a shop full of robots in assorted states of repair, need an *organic* slave as well as all his mechanical ones? It is never made very clear what kind of work Shmi Skywalker does for her master; her only function in the plot is to be *owned,* and to make her son grieve when he is separated from her. One wonders why she would be allowed to have a robot to help her at all. Why not just have the robot, and dispense with the human slave?

Suppose we let all this pass. Why, then, did Anakin build a *protocol* droid? Surely, if your mother were a maid-of-all-work and you wanted to build a machine to help her, you would not immediately think of making a slow-moving mechanical man who was 'fluent in over six million forms of communication'. Owen Lars, in the original *Star Wars,* had no need for an interpreter; he bought C-3PO from an obvious fence, presumably at a bargain price, to talk sense into his moisture vaporators. But apparently Shmi, a scrap dealer's slave on the same unimportant desert world, *does* need a translator; needs one so badly that her son decides to make her one out of spare parts as the ideal gift. It does not begin to be plausible; it hardly even pretends to be.

But these are side issues. The crucial fault, of course, is that young Anakin (as we, the audience, know in advance) will turn out to be Darth Vader; and yet, when they meet face to face after a lapse of many years, neither will recognize the other. Lucas made an attempt to save the appearances in Episode III, where Threepio's memory is wiped. Even devoted fans of the series admit that this is clumsy. So why was it done this way at all?

The only answer appears to be that Lucas wanted C-3PO in all six episodes, and he needed a way to shoehorn him into *Phantom* – a film that otherwise had no need of him. So he gave him a cameo in the first place he could think of. This, surely, was a case that cried out for some creative discomfort. Lucas settled for a lazy idea when it would have been much easier, and immeasurably better artistically, to sweat over the problem until he came up with a good idea.

Before I sat down to write this *essai,* I spent a few minutes brainstorming for ideas on how better to introduce Threepio in Episode I. By your leave, I will offer the one that seemed to work best – the one that solved the most problems in the story. I don't claim that it is the best possible idea; it is merely the most interesting of several that occurred to me when I troubled to *think* about the problem. Here it is:

What if C-3PO was a protocol droid working for the Trade Federation? We see an almost identical droid (silver, not gold) in the opening scene aboard the Trade Federation flagship; it's the one that serves drinks to Qui-Gon and Obi-Wan while they wait in the conference room. This would improve the story in several ways. To begin with, it would give some personality to the protocol droid in the conference room – a scene that desperately needed something to make it interesting. It would give the two Jedi a better motive for going down to Naboo. Their stated motive is nonsense: you can't warn somebody that an invasion fleet is coming by stowing away on the invasion fleet itself. But as a protocol droid, Threepio would have been a witness to the machinations that led the Trade Federation leaders to the brink of treason and open war. That information could have been vital to the Naboo side, and politically important to the Republic itself, and to the Jedi Council.

One can easily imagine the two Jedi taking Threepio by force, removing the restraining bolt that his previous master presumably gave him, and using him to bluff their way through to a shuttle that would take them down to Naboo. Threepio would likely have helped them, moved by a combination of gratitude (they set him free of the restraining bolt and some unsavoury owners) and timidity (these are, after all, Jedi, and we see them using the Force to smash droids into kindling). On Naboo he would have met R2-D2, who was assigned to the Queen's yacht. They would have been a robotic Montague and Capulet; much could have been made of the process by which they learnt to work together, and turned from official enemies into bickering but steadfast friends.

This kind of comic relief was something Lucas knew how to write and direct; the byplay between the droids is one of the best things in the original *Star Wars,* and indeed they carry the action all by themselves for much of the first act. That suggests the best reason of all for introducing C-3PO this way: it would have cut Jar-Jar Binks completely out of the story. The idea of Jar-Jar was not fundamentally a bad one, but the execution was embarrassing. He introduces an element of the lowest slapstick into otherwise serious, or at least seriocomic, scenes; and Lucas simply has not got the skills to handle slapstick. Physical humour is a 'low' form of comedy, in that it makes few demands on the intelligence of its audience; but it requires tremendous technical skill to do properly. Charlie Chaplin and Buster Keaton were enormously respected by their fellow actors, who knew how hard it was to make people laugh in that way.

Episode II sees Lucas resorting to more and more implausible devices to rescue himself from his own hasty decisions. The movie scarcely hangs together at all: the characters go rabbiting all over the Galaxy on slight pretexts, and in consequence, have little time to interact with one another. What this episode *should* have done – what it needed to accomplish – was to show Anakin growing into an idealistic young Jedi knight, 'the best star pilot in the galaxy', and 'a good friend', as Obi-Wan called him in the original. The romance between Anakin and Padme could have been deferred to Episode III; or it could have been made a complication in the second act of *Clones,* a wedge that came between Obi-Wan and his apprentice.

But here again, Lucas took the easiest way out. Instead of *showing* us these things, he simply *told* us – in the most static and unconvincing way, by having Anakin and Obi-Wan reminisce about their adventures together for a minute or two in a moving lift. The adventure they alluded to would have made a splendid overture to the main story. It would have served the same function (and could have been about the same length) as the battle of Hoth in *Empire* or the Jabba the Hutt section of *Jedi*. That would have put the characters, especially Anakin, on a firm footing, and given the audience a solid impression of Anakin as a good guy. Instead, our first long look at the grown-up Anakin comes in static indoor scenes, where he paces up and down and complains incessantly about Obi-Wan to anyone who will sit still for it. He comes across as a whiny, spoilt adolescent, self-important, consumed with petty grievances, but too cowardly to complain to Obi-Wan himself. This is a *disastrous* error. It undermines the whole character of Anakin; we almost feel that his turning to the Dark Side is redundant. Lucas, in his own mind, firmly believed that the story arc of the prequels was about the good and virtuous Anakin being seduced by evil. But the good and virtuous Anakin only existed in Lucas's mind. He never made it into the films.

Let us finish off with an example from Episode III: the death of Padme, which is a crucial point in the plot. We have a world in which the most hideously maimed and broken men can be put together again with prosthetic parts. We see it done with Anakin, who loses all four of his limbs, has the skin burnt off the rest of his body by hot lava – *and lives.* He is rebuilt into the dark and menacing form of Darth Vader. And yet Padme, having what (as far as we can tell) is a perfectly ordinary pregnancy, lying in an aseptic delivery room, surrounded by droid doctors and the best medical technology in the nascent Empire, can die in childbirth – not even from eclampsia or an infection, but simply from a broken heart. Women do die in childbirth sometimes, even with advanced medicine, and it is at least debatable that some women die of broken hearts; but never the two in combination. The presence of a newborn child concentrates the instincts and the affections wonderfully; it gives the most broken-hearted mother something to live for. Worst of all, Anakin has just turned to the Dark Side specifically to learn how to *prevent* Padme's death – and yet he does absolutely nothing about it.

Once again, a few minutes' thought suggested a number of alternatives to me; here is the one I personally like best. Lucas himself almost stumbled into it – but instead of filming it, he made it a lie told by the Emperor. When the newly built Vader takes his first lurching steps (so painfully reminiscent of *Frankenstein*), he asks what has happened to Padme. 'You killed her,' says the Emperor. Very well: What if Anakin really *did* kill Padme? How would that come about?

We know that Anakin saw little of Padme during her pregnancy – the Jedi and the Emperor kept him too busy, and usually too far away. On the evidence of Vader's dialogue in *Jedi*, he never knew that she was carrying twins. Let us suppose, then, that Padme is safely delivered of her two children while Anakin was away; that she knows he has turned to the Dark Side and is now the Emperor's apprentice. What does she do? The obvious thing is to hide the children. She places Luke in the care of Anakin's kinsman, Owen Lars – on the face of it, a fearfully stupid thing to do, for Vader knows that place all too well. But we may suppose that she works out her plan with Obi-Wan, and he chooses to go into retirement on Tattooine specifically to watch over the boy and protect him from the Empire. Then she hides Leia by having her adopted into the powerful Organa family on Alderaan.

At this point, both her children are in safe places, and all the witnesses are in hiding as well. (Except the droids in the delivery room; but she could have had their memories wiped, and we would be much more willing to accept it than we were with a known and beloved character like Threepio.) The only really dangerous witness – the first one Vader would seek out and interrogate – is now Padme herself. So she gets on her fancy ship with a skeleton crew, devoted family retainers who will join her on a suicide mission – and goes to seek out the command ship on which, even then, Vader and the Emperor are searching for her. She goes to meet her fate, and challenge it. Either the Emperor will die, and the threat will be ended, or she will die, and her children's secret will be safe.

The final scene would be very short: it would fall like a hammer blow to the vitals. There might be a short radio conversation between Vader and Padme while her ship locks in a collision course with his. 'I can't let the Republic die,' she might say. '*You* can't let the Jedi die, Ani. Search your feelings!' (When you are conducting a life-or-death negotiation and every second counts, the dialogue can afford to be on the nose.) The Emperor looks on, unconcerned and sneering: he knows how strong the Dark Side is, and what chains of shared guilt bind his new apprentice to him. We see Vader on the bridge as the ship approaches in the viewport. He looks back and forth between the Emperor and his wife, indecisive – as he will one day look between the Emperor and Luke. But *this* time, he is not strong enough; he capitulates. At the last possible moment, he gives the weapons officer the order to open fire, and Padme's ship is obliterated. Cut to an exterior shot of the command ship, bits of burning metal glancing off the hull. On the soundtrack, we hear Vader's cry of loss and grief, and the Emperor's triumphant laughter.

This scenario, or something like it, would give Padme *something to do,* instead of being a stereotypical damsel in distress, and dying pointlessly of a broken heart. We could believe that a firebrand like Leia could be the daughter of such a mother. (Natalie Portman could have prepared for the role by carefully watching Leia's scenes in *A New Hope,* and adopting similar mannerisms.) It would set up a resonance with the ending of Episode VI. Lucas is very fond of such resonances: he exploited them incessantly, even shamelessly, in the prequels. 'Each stanza sort of rhymes with the last,' as he puts it. The ending of *Jedi* would appear in a whole new light: Vader's second chance, which he thought would never come: an opportunity to redeem his failure when Padme needed him most. Lucas had the right idea, or part of it, when he thought of making things rhyme. But rhyme in poetry is most effective at the end of a line. The word that rhymes is also the last word.

Those, at any rate, are the ideas: they took me all of fifteen minutes' creative discomfort – much less time to invent them than it took to write them down. I have no doubt that Lucas could have come up with better ones than these if he had seriously tried. But he was too used to making snap decisions and having them obeyed. Lucasfilm had become his perfect machine, a machine that incorporated hundreds of talented men and women in its works; a machine that would instantly do, not what he wanted done, but what he *told* it to do – as literal-minded as a computer. The days when he worked with equals, like Coppola, Spielberg, Kurtz, or Kasdan, were long gone; now he had only subordinates, too timid to question him, too small in stature to challenge him to do better. With such servants, his own capacity for creative discomfort atrophied and, I fear, eventually died. And to a great extent, the *Star Wars* prequels died along with it, leaving behind only a gigantic mausoleum of bloodless fight scenes and visual effects. They could have done so much more. They could have *lived*.

AD EFFIGIEM:

THE STRAWMAN FALLACY IN UTOPIAN FICTION

Of all the habitual fallacies and prejudices that have poisoned the wells of reason in our time, none, perhaps, has been so destructive as what Owen Barfield christened 'chronological snobbery'. This is the strange belief that modern ideas and habits, simply because they are modern, are inherently superior to those of former times. This belief has become so prevalent that it is now recognized as a category of informal fallacy in itself.

This snobbery is perhaps the last remaining vestige or outcrop of the once formidable massif of Victorian optimism. The belief in the inevitability of progress was dealt a crushing blow by the First World War, and even the belief in progress itself was drastically undermined by the rank flowering of cultural and moral relativism that took its shallow root in the decades after 1960. The Victorians were chronological snobs because they thought themselves the first geniuses on the earth, the evolutionary apex of a long history of fools. Modern relativists, in my experience, are chronological snobs because they believe we are *all* fools. Denying even the possibility of genius, they refuse to take lessons from a lot of uppity dead white men who think they have something to teach.

But whether you arrive at this position by the high road of egotism or the low road of relativism, the result is the same, and fatal to the reasoning faculty. Any other fallacy can be disproved by argument and evidence.

Chronological snobbery will not hear the arguments, because they are the arguments of dead men. It will not look at the evidence, because the evidence is old. At bottom I suppose it is a cognitive disorder, somewhat akin to paranoia. The paranoiac believes everyone is conspiring against him, and cannot be persuaded otherwise, because everyone who tries to talk him out of his delusion is obviously part of the conspiracy. The snob believes everyone who disagrees with him is stupid, and cannot be persuaded otherwise, because everyone who tries to talk him out of it is a fool by definition.

If you read ancient or mediaeval books with real attention, or even look at ancient artefacts in a museum, you will quickly realize how little human beings have changed in the last five thousand years. Last Saturday, for instance, I went to see an exhibit of Egyptian art at the Glenbow Museum in Calgary. It contained many second-rate or merely utilitarian pieces, which is the common fate of museum exhibits in provincial market towns, but that gave it a peculiar strength that could easily be lost in a first-class display. It was not in the least striking; in fact, it was striking for not being striking. It was fantastic in its ordinariness, like a Chestertonian *Mooreeffoc* turned inside-out.

People commonly go to Egyptian exhibits to see all the uncanny things the Egyptians did with their dead, stuffing sarcophagi with mummies and canopic jars with their entrails. The exhibit at the Glenbow was lacking in mummies, though it had some jars still said to hold the residue of their ancient contents. What it had instead, and that in abundance, was an assortment of bowls, jars, bottles, mirrors, board games, jewellery, knick-knacks, and impedimenta, such as you might find in any high-toned department store or curio-shop. Unlike a lot of later civilizations, the Egyptians had a taste for simplicity in small household items. Many of the things they made were indistinguishable from modern articles, except that they lacked the queer hieroglyphic inscription, MADE IN CHINA.

Likewise, when I went to the Field Museum in Chicago last July, and set eyes upon the string-seated chair from the tomb of Yuya and Tjuya, I felt myself in the awful presence of the Grandfather of Bauhaus. Apart from the gilding and the carvings on the side and back panels, I could probably order a virtually identical chair from this year's IKEA catalogue. The materials and the manufacturing process have changed, but in three thousand years we have made no improvement at all in the art of supporting the human bum.

But chronological snobs do not look at Egyptian furniture and housewares. If they go to such exhibits at all, it is to goggle at the burial gear and snigger at the superstitious fools who believed such queer things about the afterlife. This is only human, after all. The human nervous system is designed to notice change before continuity and differences before similarities. From a merely practical standpoint, a moving tiger is an object of much more immediate importance than a stationary tree. But the tree is more useful in the long run. We tend to see the tiger and ignore the landscape; and we see the showy and meretricious differences between Egyptian culture and our own, while being inexcusably blind to the limitless background of similarity.

It is this peculiar historical blindness that lets us ignore the obvious lessons of the past, even when put in plain English by the genius of Jonathan Swift. Some of Swift's criticisms of humanity seem very modern indeed: and we, snobs that we are, pay him the patronizing tribute of calling him 'ahead of his time'. In truth his time had nothing to do with the case. There were millions of human beings in the eighteenth century who were incapable of seeing Man as Swift saw him, and there are millions today. There was only one Swift then, and today there is none. We have thousands of derivative thinkers who think Swift's views are childishly obvious, because they read *Gulliver's Travels* as children, or saw the book traduced on film, or – most likely of all – were influenced by still other thinkers who had read Swift. His ideas have become the common property of our culture, and we can appreciate them without having the genius to invent them.

Among his other talents, Swift was a past master of what is sometimes called the fallacy of the straw man. He could use it to make a point or bamboozle an audience, and he could also see through it. Indeed, he seems to have had an intuitive understanding of a larger class of fallacies of which the straw man is only the most obvious example. This is from Part III of *Gulliver*, a shot at the ivory-tower savants of Laputa:

> What I ... thought altogether unaccountable, was the strong Disposition I observed in them towards News and Politics, perpetually inquiring into Public Affairs, giving their judgements in Matters of State, and passionately disputing every Inch of a Party Opinion. I have, indeed, observed the same Disposition among most of the Mathematicians I have known in *Europe*, though I could never discover the least Analogy between the two Sciences; unless those People suppose, that, because the smallest Circle hath as many Degrees as the largest, therefore the Regulation and Management of the World require no more Abilities, than the Handling and Turning of a Globe.

George Orwell, who quotes this passage in 'Politics vs. Literature', makes it out as an attack on scientists in general, and actually accuses Swift of lacking imagination. But it is a shrewd and honest observation on Swift's part. The world is full of would-be Technocrats. Half the political theorists one hears of are themselves neither politicians nor political scientists, but monists turned monomaniacs, cranks peddling panaceas. They construct their own globes and turn them prettily, and imagine that this qualifies them to regulate the world. Rousseau, Shelley, Marx, Tolstoy, Rand, Chomsky, and a hundred others made their names this way. Each one comes up with one great Idea, and pretends that it can explain everything else. Every ideologue, as such, is a prey to this weakness, and every ideology is a ghastly oversimplification. The Marxist says that everything is class struggle, and produces the Gulag. The Nazi says that everything is racial struggle, and produces the Holocaust. The Wahhabist says that everything is religious struggle, and produces suicide bombers and blood-soaked ruins. Every Utopian scheme of the world is a pyramid scheme, and its natural product is a pyramid of corpses.

Of course, every one of these ideologies works brilliantly on paper. Class struggle cannot make the world go round, but it can make a globe go round. And the globe, or the paper Utopia, is itself a kind of straw man; more precisely, a straw world. The object is not to demolish it, as we do with the straw men we make of our opponents' views, but to perfect it; but the fallacy is exactly the same. It accounts for the weakness of the opposing case, but not for its strength. The most important thing about a globe is not that it resembles the earth, but that it is not the earth. The most important thing about a Utopia is not that the world might have been Utopian, but that it is not Utopian. The globe, or the Utopia, accounts for everything about the world, except for the qualities that make it real.

In Swift's time, Latin was still the language of the philosophers, so I find it fitting to give this class of fallacies a Latin name. I shall call it the *argumentum ad effigiem* – the argument to the effigy. When we burn a man in effigy, we are quite literally burning a straw man. The fallacy lies in believing that the real man is as combustible as the straw man, or, after the effigy is burnt, that the real man is as dead as the straw man.

You might think that even human beings would be clever enough to see the silliness of these beliefs, but you would be mistaken. The clichéd apparatus of the voodoo doll is an exercise in arguing to the effigy. The magician sticks pins in his straw man, and expects the real man to double over in pain. I have heard that this practice does not occur in the genuine religion or magic of Vodoun. In one way, this does not matter, for the idea exists somewhere. In another way, it is the strongest evidence for the power of the idea. The conception of the voodoo doll has such a grip on our imagination that we have to father it onto a lot of unoffending Haitians, and so absolve ourselves of inventing it. But in fact human beings of every culture have some form of belief in sympathetic magic. It seems to require a special effort of the intellect not to believe in it. We feel that in some mystical sense the voodoo doll exemplifies the way things ought to work. And as soon as we transport this idea into the abstract realm, we are apt to imagine that it really does work. Otherwise we could not believe that demolishing the straw-man argument has any effect on the real one.

Another classic form of the *argumentum ad effigiem* is what Northrop Frye calls the ironic mode in literature. Ironic fiction depends upon the conceit that the characters in the story are inferior in kind, or at least in mental capacity, to the author and his audience. In other words, it depends on making one's characters into straw men, instead of making them behave like real people. The fact that ironic writers (and the critics who worship them) think of themselves as the only true realists under the canopy, and dismiss everyone else as romantics and escapists, merely shows what nonsensical meanings have become attached to the word *realism*. It is somehow 'realistic' to write about ugliness, but not about beauty; about cowardice, but not courage; about villains, but not heroes. Yet everyone with a normal aesthetic sense and a little inclination to travel (instead of seeing the world through the distorting eye of television) can see that nature contains far more beauty than ugliness; and everyone who has a nodding acquaintance with human beings knows that genuine villains are as rare as genuine saints.

Catch-22 is a famous example of the ironic novel, and it answers neatly to the charge of *ad effigiem*. It captures (and very well, too) the empire-building, favour-currying, shallow and stupid and officious side of army life; but it leaves out the bravery, the selflessness, the patriotism and public spirit without which no army would ever fight. It is true that armies have sometimes been composed largely of mercenaries; but no mercenary force ever put up with the malicious incompetence of Heller's generals. A man who fights for a noble cause will endure all kinds of hardships that he would not tolerate for a moment if he were fighting for money. In the end Yossarian runs away, because he, like every other character in the book, is not a man but a mannequin. He has been stripped of every noble human quality, and has no will to fight for anything but his own personal survival. He is, in fact, what C.S. Lewis called a man without a chest; and so *Catch-22*, comic masterpiece though it is, is a novel without a heart.

When fantasy first became established as a commercial genre, it was solidly grounded in Frye's category of the romantic. This is one of many reasons why critics of the Moorcock school hate Tolkien and all his imitators. In one sense, all their calls for subversion in fantasy are really calls for the ironic, because what they most want to subvert is the idea of human dignity. Elric is an ironic hero, a classic anti-hero in fact: a spiritual (and almost literal) vampire, devoid of morals; motivated by selfishness, a consuming hatred of his own people, and mere contempt for everyone else. Miéville's New Crobuzon is notoriously ironic, a city where everything is ugly, everyone acts from the crassest motives, and from which nature itself has been so thoroughly expunged that no green and growing thing has ever been found there. The irony of their school is the deliberate antithesis to the romance of Tolkien and his followers.

It is no accident that Moorcock and Miéville set up Mervyn Peake as the anti-Tolkien, the principal god of their degraded pantheon. Much as I admire the technical skill Peake showed in *Titus Groan,* and to a lesser degree in *Gormenghast,* I cannot help but see that all his work is disfigured by the relentless irony that those others so admire.

The tone is set on the very first page. *Titus Groan* begins with a description of the room where the prize-winning works of the Bright Carvers gather dust, unseen and unappreciated, century after century. The Carvers are ironic: we snigger at them for wasting their lives making art for the denizens of Gormenghast, which nobody cares about or even looks at. The people in the castle are ironic: we shake our heads at the blatant philistines who are anaesthetic to the very best of the Carvers' work, and wilfully burn the rest. And the Earl of Groan himself is immediately established as an ironic figure, carrying on the whole ridiculous procedure for no reason of his own, but only because it is written in a book of protocol that he thoroughly resents and hardly understands.

All this is red meat and strong beer to the Moorcock school; or perhaps I should say that it is raw fish and goblin-flesh, prized because it is not 'leaves out of the elf-country, gah!' There are no heroes in *Titus Groan,* and the most vivid of all the weird and monstrous characters is Steerpike, as frank a villain as Snidely Whiplash. All the characters are monsters, and most are monsters of the same kind: their entire personality is based on a single characteristic, and a character flaw at that. For Irma Prunesquallor, the flaw is vanity; for Barquentine, slavish traditionalism; for Gertrude Groan, indifference; for Sepulchrave, Earl of Groan, depression. Cora and Clarice are pure malicious selfishness. It is all very Dickensian, or rather sub-Dickensian, because Dickens at least sometimes gave his characters good qualities, and he nearly always gave them some scope to exercise their natures for good or ill. Most of Peake's monsters are comically ineffectual; they are comical precisely because they are ineffectual. Irma cannot find anyone to feed her voracious appetite for flattery; Barquentine cannot stop things from happening that do not occur in the book of rituals; Cora and Clarice are so imbecilic that they cannot even think of setting fire to their brother's library without Steerpike's help. Steerpike himself is a straw man, but he at least is stuffed with a better grade of straw. His defining flaw is ambition, and he finds scope for it by exploiting the other straw men's weaknesses, and so makes the entire plot go.

Some critics have said that the ruinous castle of Gormenghast is a metaphor for the human mind, and the vivid monstrosities that inhabit it are the urges of the primitive id, dragged into the light of at least minimal self-consciousness. This kind of Freudian analysis is out of style nowadays, and in any case Peake was not writing a straightforward allegory of human psychology. The best of his characters – Steerpike, Alfred Prunesquallor, Gertrude in her rare moments of furious energy – rise above the status of mere hypostatized qualities, and almost become persons in their own right.

Other commentators see Gormenghast as a parody of modern civilization. This interpretation is favoured strongly in the BBC miniseries. Warren Mitchell, who turned in a brilliantly grotesque performance as Barquentine, suggested that the endless rituals of Gormenghast were equivalent to the nonsensical traditions and religious superstitions of Europe at the opening of the twentieth century. Sebastian Peake, the author's son, says that the resemblance is rather with the decaying and ritual-encrusted Confucian society of imperial China. Mervyn Peake was born in China in the very month when the last Emperor was overthrown, and saw the disintegration of that society at first hand.

Whatever the source, the 'thinning' (to borrow John Clute's term) of Gormenghast reflects the dissolution of traditional societies all over the world during Peake's lifetime. During or after the First World War, people all over the industrialized countries woke up, in a sense, from their post-Victorian dream, and realized that many of the things they had been telling themselves about the world were lies. Some went further and thought they must all be lies. These became Surrealists, or Dadaists, or nihilists. Some clung to this or that apocalyptic would-be prophet, and became Marxists, Fascists, Anarchists, and so *ad nauseam*. Others retreated into vulgar hedonism, or 'art for art's sake', or – the most common response of all – tried to ignore what was happening around them and cling to their traditions as best they could. And all these kinds of people have their counterparts in Gormenghast.

But there is something strange in holding up Gormenghast as a mirror of contemporary society. It is at best a distorting mirror, a funhouse mirror. A funhouse mirror exaggerates the ugliness of a face, and turns even beauty into ugliness by robbing it of its proper proportions; and so it is with Gormenghast. There is no hint in the books that the endless rituals of the castle ever had any practical purpose or justification, or that anyone was better off for observing them. This is a curiously one-eyed view of tradition. Christianity began as a desperate campaign to save human souls from their own worst impulses, and for all the faults of the churches, it serves that function still. The rule of law, for all its byzantine absurdities and blatant injustices, still protects people against the worst caprices of private vengeance and public tyranny. Confucianism at its best provided a government of royal philosophers, who are one degree better than philosopher-kings, because the king was not required to be a philosopher himself. If it later degenerated into a make-work scheme for self-seeking academics, it was an indictment of human weakness and not of Confucius' maxims of government. Gormenghast lived and died by straw rituals – empty of content and purpose, and stuffed with implausible rubbish to plump them out and give them the shape of real ones. A society of straw men would naturally have straw rituals, but there is no particular reason why such a society should exist at all.

This is the cardinal weakness of Gormenghast, as of every *ad effigiem* model of human life. Warren Mitchell likes to fancy that the rituals of Gormenghast are empty because all ritual is empty. In fact, they are empty because Gormenghast itself is empty. If straw men worship straw gods, that does not invalidate worship; at most, it invalidates straw, at least as a material for men and gods. You can knock the stuffing out of a straw world, but that does not prove that you can knock the stuffing out of the real world. The analogy breaks down precisely because the real world is not stuffed. The resemblance of a straw man to a real one is merely formal; and while form is important, it is not everything. The content of a human being, or a ritual, or a world, matters at least as much as its shape.

For after all, there are worse things than straw men. There are also hollow men. T. S. Eliot wrote about hollow men, and as Orwell said in 'Inside the Whale', achieved 'the difficult feat of making modern life out to be worse than it is'. An argument, or a character in a novel, or a globe, can be filled with nothing but hot air. Some of Ayn Rand's most characteristic productions could be demolished by sticking a pin in them. These kinds of arguments are especially dangerous, not because they themselves are likely to take anyone in, but because they may persuade the inexperienced that *all* argument consists of exactly the same kind of humbug. This is a real danger, as the history of Postmodernism has shown.

It is, after all, the most natural thing in the world, if you have tested half a dozen apparently solid objects and found them to be nothing more than balloons, to assume that every object of that kind is a balloon, and to disbelieve in the very idea of solidity. The Amazing Randi has constructed an entire ideology of his own on this belief. CSICOP has dwindled in stature since its heyday in the 1970s, when there really was an astounding amount of hot air filling out the forms of supernatural belief; and that is partly because some of the balloons Randi tried to prick really were solid objects, and blunted the point of his pin.

The essence of Randi's method is to show that a thing can be falsified, and take this as proof that it *was* falsified. He 'proved' that Uri Geller's spoon-bending trick was a fake by showing how he could fake it himself. Since Geller did happen to be a fake, this earned Randi an unjustified reputation as a debunker. In fact, Randi's method is merely the elementary logical fallacy of affirming the consequent. The fallacy takes this form:

> If Uri Geller bends a spoon with his hands, the spoon will be bent.
> The spoon is bent.
> Therefore, Geller bent it with his hands.

So far, so good. Now let us apply the same method to other premises.

> If you induce hallucinations in a subject's brain, he will have a religious experience.
> John has had a religious experience.
> Therefore, John was hallucinating.

> If you make a subject act on post-hypnotic suggestion, she will attribute the act to her own free will.
> Anne attributes her actions to her own free will.
> Therefore, Anne has been acting on post-hypnotic suggestions.

These arguments are in fact in daily use to discredit religious experience and the notion of free will. It is now fashionable among skeptics to claim that there is a 'God gene' which causes people to believe in a deity; and there is a whole school of psychologists who eagerly propound the idea that free will is an illusion manufactured by the brain *after* it performs a predetermined action.

Now consider these arguments:

> If you induce visual hallucinations in a subject's brain, he will see a light.
> Paul sees a light.

Therefore, Paul is hallucinating.

If you make a counterfeit of a $20 bill, it will look like real money.
This $20 bill looks like real money.
Therefore, the bill is a counterfeit.

These arguments are obviously bogus. We all know that there are in fact such things as real lights and real money. The fact that they can be counterfeited or hallucinated is no proof that they do not exist. Indeed, it is strong evidence that they *do* exist. If there were no real lights, we should be unable to recognize the hallucinations as appearances of light; we would not even have a word for light. If there were no real twenty-dollar bills, nobody would have any reason to make false ones. Counterfeiters do not commonly try to pass banknotes worth seven grizzles or fifteen grozzles. Someone did once successfully pass some Canadian twenty-dollar bills with the portrait of the Queen replaced by a topless picture of Claudia Schiffer. This is not evidence against the existence of money, but rather *for* the existence of human stupidity. The boy who accepted the bogus bills tried to pass them on to someone else on the midway where he worked, and chose a victim less idiotic than himself – such persons being easy enough to find. He was arrested, charged, and fired from his job. But there are no monetary skeptics building a theory of amonetism on such incidents, as theological skeptics build theories of atheism.

Affirming the consequent is only valid in logic when the conditional statement takes the form, not of *If P then Q*, but of *If **and only if** P, then Q*. A twenty-dollar bill may look like money because it is money. Paul may see a light because the sun is shining on him. Joan of Arc may have had religious experiences because God or an angel really did talk to her. Even poor Uri Geller may have bent the spoons without using his hands. There are plenty of other ways to bend spoons without invoking telekinetic powers to explain them. For all we know, it may actually be possible to bend spoons by telekinesis; at any rate, we could not disprove it by

Randi's argument. He simply assumes, without any kind of proof, that the way *he* did it is the only way it can be done.

It is really rather amazing how many logical errors Randi packs into that one demonstration. He affirms the consequent. He constructs a straw man, or if you will allow me the conceit, an *argumentum ad effigiem*. He is guilty of *petitio principii*, better known as 'arguing in a circle', because he brings to his case the very assumption (that telekinesis is impossible) which he professes to derive from it. He typically presents his case with all kinds of rhetorical handwaving, including the appeal to ridicule and the abusive *argumentum ad hominem*. His whole method is a tissue of lies, made plausible by one poor thread of truth: that Geller is in fact a charlatan. He wants you to come out of his rhetorical maze convinced that Geller is a phony, without ever noticing the far more important and striking fact that Randi himself is a phony.

The *ad effigiem* attack in *Titus Groan* and *Gormenghast*, being looser and more rhetorical, does not easily lend itself to being expressed in a syllogism, even a faulty one. It boils down roughly to this:

> All rituals have resemblances to the rituals of Gormenghast.
> The rituals of Gormenghast are pointless.
> Therefore, all rituals are pointless.

The first premise is true by definition, or we should not apply the word *rituals* to what went on at Gormenghast. But the premises in no way justify the conclusion, for nobody has established *how* the rituals of Gormenghast resemble others. It is only assumed that pointlessness must be one of the points of resemblance. This is partly the fallacy of converse accident – assuming that what is true of one example is true in all cases. Cats are mammals, and cats have kittens, but that does not mean all mammals have kittens.

When the example itself is fictitious, it does not prove that the 'accidents' are true even in one case. I could say that zeffles are mammals, and zeffles eat gwermwims. That does not prove that all mammals eat gwermwims, or even that any mammals eat gwermwims. It does not prove anything at all, because I just made it up. Likewise, Peake just made up Gormenghast and its meaningless rituals, and from it you cannot infer anything about real rituals. The error of converse accident is combined with the fallacy of the straw man. Peake's misguided admirers pile a fictitious Pelion upon a bogus Ossa, and think they have overtopped the real and solid rock of Olympus. All Utopian literature (and anti-Utopian literature, for that matter) is essentially a game of feeding fictitious gwermwims to imaginary zeffles. We are meant to draw inferences about real things and people from examples that do not even exist, or much resemble the real things they are supposed to be patterned after.

When I mention anti-Utopian literature in this connection, you will probably think of *Nineteen Eighty-Four,* and wonder where it fits in. In fact there is very little of the straw man in Orwell's dystopian masterpiece. The mindless worship of Big Brother was derived from Stalin's 'cult of personality' and the equally grotesque Führer-worship in Nazi Germany. The tortures and inquisitions of the Thought Police were based on his real experiences in the Spanish Civil War. The Ministry of Truth was based on the Ministry of Information, in which Orwell worked during the Second World War, and its grotesque output of lies and forgeries was patterned after the impossible gyrations that loyal Communists were expected to perform with every change of Party line. Even the dreary details of life in a bombed-out London were extrapolated, almost without exaggeration, from the dreary London of the post-war years, when the damage of the V1 bombs had not yet been repaired, and the wartime rationing of necessities was still largely in place. Even something as fantastic as the Party's claim that two and two could make five if they wished it was based on a real event: the alleged fulfilment by the U.S.S.R. of the First Five-Year Plan in only four years, for which the Soviets made '2+2=5' a celebratory slogan.

But even Orwell sometimes left hollow places in his work, or stuffed the interstices with straw. His work is weakest where it is most imaginative. He did an impressive job of welding together the disparate totalitarianisms of Germany, Italy, Russia and Spain, and the Nosey-Parker officiousness of wartime England, to produce an apparently monolithic composite. But it is only an apparent monolith, for the cracks are hastily papered over with the vague and incomplete ideology of Ingsoc. We are told that the Party desired power purely for its own sake, and consequently had none of the liberal illusions that were the undoing of earlier tyrants. In fact, nobody ever built a mass movement on the pure lust for power.

In Russia, to take the best example, people would work for the dictatorship of the proletariat only because they did not understand that it would be a real dictatorship, with a real dictator who was even less inclined than the Tsars to share his power. Stalin said in public that he was working for international Socialism and brotherhood and the betterment of the Russian people. The *nomenklatura* knew better, but that does not mean that they shared or even understood Stalin's real motives. When he died, Stalin left behind a massive system of total oppression, and no particular reason to use it. None of his successors wanted that power to exist for its own sake; at minimum, they wanted to possess it for themselves. In the old Communist phrase, it was a question of WHO oppressed WHOM; and Stalin's heirs had no intention of becoming the WHOM. But that meant that they let parts of the Stalinist machine rust, and even dismantled those that were most likely to be dangerous to themselves. There were no more great Party purges after Stalin died. In the end the *nomenklatura* lost their devotion to the Party, and at last even their ruthlessness, and the breakup of the system became inevitable. Orwell misses all that, because he replaces the real motives of a ruling class with the straw motive of pure power.

As I said at the beginning of this *essai*, Jonathan Swift was a past master of the *argumentum ad effigiem*, three hundred years before I gave it that name. Part IV of *Gulliver's Travels* is a massive straw man, or straw Yahoo, and it is also a parody of the straw Utopias that were already infesting the literary and political landscape. Like so many others, Swift's argument can be simplified into a cracked syllogism:

All men look like men.
All Yahoos look like men.
Therefore, all men are Yahoos.

The Yahoos are a gross and obscene distortion of humanity, with all the human vices and none of the human virtues. Of course, in pointing this out, I am simply inviting an *ad hominem* attack. It will be said that I am a Yahoo myself, and ashamed of the fact, and trying to cover it up by attributing nonexistent virtues to myself. I have seen exactly the same attack made upon others, and have no reason to expect that I will be spared. Suffice it to say that if I were a Yahoo, I would not be ashamed of it; because shame is not an emotion that the Yahoos were represented as having.

In fact this attack is based squarely, but not soundly, on an *ad effigiem* argument. The Yahoos are *like* men, but they are *not* men; Swift makes this explicit, though the Houyhnhnms, blinded by prejudice, are unable to see the difference. Yahoos have no art, no science, no philosophy, no morality, no altruism, no finer emotions, no architecture, no technology, no trade, and apparently not much in the way of language. In these things they rather resemble baboons. But no baboon is ambitious, or avaricious, or manipulative; baboons do not fight wars or set up tyrannical governments. The Yahoos do. They are a vicious engraftment of human follies onto a merely animal intelligence, and the offence is compounded by putting the resulting hybrid in an apparently human body. In fact an animal as stupid as a Yahoo would be incapable of conceiving the higher forms of human wickedness. Avarice arises from trade, lying arises from language, war and tyranny arise from the art of government. I do not mean that these evils are inevitable growths; I mean that they cannot grow at all without the good things upon which they depend. Language is a necessary but not a sufficient precondition for lying: an animal without language has nothing to tell liescwith. In short, the sins attributed to the Yahoos are beyond their ability to perform or even to comprehend.

On the other hand, or hoof, we have the straw Utopia of the Houyhnhnms. Their lives are governed by a 'Reason' as rigid and meaningless as the rituals of Gormenghast. They seem to have no desires or emotions at all. They practise eugenics in a purely negative sense, not rearing any offspring that is not a perfectly representative Houyhnhnm. They have no word for *lie*, but also no word for *argument*. They have no hate, but also no love, except for a sort of abstract goodwill towards everything in nature (except the Yahoos). They are, in fact, very like Vulcans, because they derive their philosophy from the same shallow Continental rationalism that Roddenberry mined for his curious notions of 'logic'. The Utopia of the Houyhnhnms would be a dreary place indeed, impossible for human beings to live in (and not only because of their physical resemblance to Yahoos). It is inhuman in every sense of the word, except that of being inhumane.

But half the intellectuals of Europe in Swift's time had visions of some such Utopia dancing in their heads. It was the Age of Reason, the Enlightenment, the age of neoclassicism, self-restraint, distrust of the emotions, and appalling poetry made up of perfectly balanced clauses set in heroic couplets. Pope's *Essay on Man*, with its endless vista of bumper-sticker mottoes, as monotonous as telegraph poles along a prairie railway, was not a typical product of Augustan poetry; it was the very best the Augustans had to offer. Gulliver was taken in by the 'reason' of the Houyhnhnms, and considered himself a Yahoo because he could not live by it, as much as for any merely physical resemblance. In the end he reacted by going mad, which in those extreme circumstances was probably the only sane thing to do. Many critics and commentators have thought that Swift was every bit the misanthrope that he caused Gulliver to become, that he really did regard all humans as Yahoos, and believed that the society of the Houyhnhnms was a model of perfection. I do not believe this for a moment. Swift did himself go mad in the end, but his insanity had fairly obvious physical causes; his mind did not die of *Weltschmerz*.

To my mind, Swift leaves the clearest cues in the concluding pages of Part IV. When Gulliver is picked up from his foundering canoe by a Portuguese ship, he is quite obviously insane, and the men who rescue him are quite obviously not Yahoos – though their kindness and concern for Gulliver's health and safety would be utterly incomprehensible to the Houyhnhnms as well. Here is a short extract:

> When they began to talk, I thought I never heard or saw any thing so unnatural; for it appeared to me as monstrous as if a Dog or a Cow should speak in *England,* or a *Yahoo* in *Houyhnhnm-Land.* The honest *Portuguese* were equally amazed at my strange Dress, and the odd Manner of delivering my Words, which however they understood very well. They spoke to me with great Humanity, and said they were sure their Captain would carry me *gratis* to *Lisbon,* from whence I might return to my own Country.... They were very curious to know my Story, but I gave them very little Satisfaction; and they all conjectured, that my Misfortunes had impaired my Reason.

A very shrewd conjecture. They take Gulliver to meet the captain:

> His Name was *Pedro de Mendez;* he was a very courteous and generous Person; he entreated me to give some Account of my self, and desired to know what I would eat or drink; said, I should be used as well as himself, and spoke so many obliging Things, that I wondered to find such Civilities from a *Yahoo.* However, I remained silent and sullen; I was ready to faint at the very Smell of him and his Men. At last I desired something to eat out of my own Canoo; but he ordered me a Chicken and some excellent Wine, and then directed that I should be put to Bed in a very clean Cabbin. I would not undress my self, but lay on the Bed-cloaths; and in half an Hour stole out, when I thought the Crew was at Dinner; and getting to the Side of the Ship, was going to leap into the Sea, and swim for my Life, rather than continue among *Yahoos.* But one of the Seamen prevented me, and having informed the Captain, I was chained to my Cabbin.

A man who would rather try to swim across the ocean than accept a lift from the friendly crew of a passing ship is not, I should venture to say, possessed of his full complement of marbles. And the 'Reason' of the Houyhnhnms, which would drive a man to such an extreme, is no very rational thing. Swift is quite capable of making Gulliver behave like a perfect idiot at times, as in his absurd bragging speech to the King of Brobdingnag; and quite obviously this is one of those times.

The edition of *Gulliver* that I have at hand has an appendix with a number of critical essays on the work. In one of these, Basil Willey says:

> Bentham, says Mill, habitually missed the truth that is in received opinions; that at any rate, I suggest, is what the satirist does and must do. He must, whether deliberately or no, miss precisely those aspects of the ignoble thing which in fact make it endurable to the non-satiric everyday eye: that is, he must ignore the *explanation* of the thing satirized – how it came to be, its history. It is a fact of experience that *tout comprendre c'est tout pardonner,* and the satirist *ex officio* cannot pardon, so he must decline to understand all and explain all. Satire is by nature non-constructive, since to construct effectively – to educate, for example, to reform, or to evangelize – one must study actual situations and actual persons in their historical setting, and this kind of study destroys the satiric approach.

There is a good deal of wisdom packed into those few sentences. Science fiction fandom in particular is full of Benthams, of poorly socialized antinomians who 'habitually miss the truth that is in received opinions'. If a commonplace belief is not immediately obvious to them, they are all too likely to reject it out of hand instead of trying to follow or reconstruct the reasoning behind it. Such persons as Moorcock and Miéville have developed this pernicious habit to a high degree. But if Swift is a satirist *ex officio*, they are satirists by vocation. Where he merely suppressed, for satirical effect, his commonsense knowledge that humans are *not* Yahoos, Moorcock and his friends refuse to accept any such knowledge in the first place. The grotesques who people New Crobuzon are not human, but a kind of urban Yahoo. The denizens of Gormenghast are not Yahoos, but they are almost as distorted as Yahoos, each one stretched to the breaking-point along his own axis of lunacy.

It would serve us very ill to take the distortions of Peake and Swift as truthful portraits of humanity, or to base our philosophies and politics on the conclusions they draw. Karl Marx invented a political system quite suitable for bees and ants, who had no need of it, but disastrously unsuitable for human beings; and the result, when others tried to put his theories into practice, was the hundred million corpses so gruesomely tallied in the *Black Book of Communism*. Taking Steerpike's attitude towards ritual, or Gulliver's attitude towards Yahoos, would be just as fatal to our sanity and well-being.

The appalling fact remains that many critics take Swift's attack on humanity at face value, and some are even convinced by it. 'Yahoo' has often been used as a term of abuse, and some people have flung it at all human beings indiscriminately. Swift built his argument on a deliberate and gigantic fallacy, or two fallacies, but he built it with such rhetorical cleverness and polemical force that thousands have taken it as earnest. Half the discussions of 'the problem of evil' that bedevil modern theology and ethics are couched in terms recognizably derived, though at many removes, from the comprehensive misanthropy of Gulliver.

We have learnt the wrong lesson from Swift, the inhuman lesson, the damning and dishonest lesson. Instead of learning to distrust straw men and Utopian arguments, we have merely learnt to construct them ourselves. I see little hope that our civilization will recover its sanity until we learn to take our lessons from the experiences of real men and women, and not from the Silly Putty distortions of professional satirists. It has taken us three hundred years to appreciate what he tried to teach us, and some of us have not understood it yet. In that sad sense, if in no other, there is some truth in the shopworn saying that Swift was ahead of his time.

WORKS CITED

Aldiss, Brian. *Report on Probability A*. London: Faber and Faber, 1968.

Bach, Richard. *Jonathan Livingston Seagull*. New York: Macmillan, 1970.

Blake, William. 'A Poison Tree'. Text online at http://www.poetryfoundation.org/poem/175222

Brooks, Terry. *The Sword of Shannara*. New York: Del Rey, 1977.

Chesterton, G. K. *Orthodoxy*. London: The Bodley Head, 1908.

Cleese, John. Talk on creativity at SMI, 1991. Video retrieved from YouTube, August, 2014, but subsequently removed.

Clute, John, and John Grant (eds.). *The Encyclopedia of Fantasy*. 1st ed. London: Orbit, 1997.

Dickens, Charles. *Our Mutual Friend*. London: Chapman & Hall, 1865.

Donaldson, Stephen R. *Lord Foul's Bane*. New York: Holt, Rinehart and Winston, 1977.

Eddings, David. *Castle of Wizardry*. New York: Del Rey, 1984.

Hancock, Niel. *Greyfax Grimwald*. New York: Popular Library, 1977.

Frye, Northrop. *Anatomy of Criticism: Four Essays*. Princeton: Princeton University Press, 1957.

Goodkind, Terry. Talk given at Borders Books in Bailey's Crossing, Va., 9 September 2000. Archived at http://web.archive.org/web/20080209010955/ http://www.prophets-inc.com/the_author/va.html

—*Naked Empire*. New York: Tor, 2003.

—*The Pillars of Creation.* New York: Tor, 2001.

—*Temple of the Winds.* New York: Tor, 1998.

—*Wizard's First Rule.* New York: Tor, 1994.

Heinlein, Robert A. *Friday.* New York: Holt, Rinehart and Winston, 1982.

Heller, Joseph. *Catch-22.* New York: Simon & Schuster, 1961.

Jones, Diana Wynne. *The Tough Guide to Fantasyland.* 1st ed. London: Vista, 1996.

Jordan, Robert. *The Eye of the World.* New York: Tor, 1990.

Kaminski, Michael. *The Secret History of Star Wars.* Kingston, Ontario: Legacy Books Press, 2008.

—Website of the same title: http://www.secrethistoryofstarwars.com

Kershner, Irvin (director), Leigh Brackett & Lawrence Kasdan (writers). *The Empire Strikes Back.* 20th Century Fox, 1980.

Lackey, Mercedes. *Magic's Pawn.* New York: DAW, 1989.

Larke, Glenda. 'Ten things I hate to see in a book meme'. Blog post, 2006. Online at http://glendalarke.blogspot.com/2006/05/ten-things-i-hate-to-see-in-a-book-meme.html

Le Guin, Ursula K. *The Language of the Night.* New York: Putnam, 1979.

Lewis, C. S. *The Horse and His Boy.* London: Geoffrey Bles, 1954.

—*Mere Christianity.* London: Geoffrey Bles, 1952.

—*The Pilgrim's Regress.* London: J. M. Dent & Sons, 1933.

Lindsay, David. *Voyage to Arcturus.* London: Methuen, 1920.

Lynd, Robert Staughton, & Helen Merrell Lynd. *Middletown: a study in contemporary American culture.* New York: Harcourt, Brace, 1929.

'Mistress Matisse'. 'A Polyamory–English Phrase Dictionary'. Blog post, 2004. Online at http://mistressmatisse.blogspot.com/2004/04/busy-girl-this-weekend.html

Mitchell, Margaret. *Gone With the Wind.* New York: Macmillan, 1936.

Orwell, George. 'Boys' Weeklies'. *Horizon,* no. 3, 1940. Online at http://www.orwell.ru/library/essays/boys/english/e_boys

—*Inside the Whale and Other Essays.* London: Victor Gollancz, 1940.

—*Nineteen Eighty-Four.* London: Secker & Warburg, 1949.

Peake, Mervyn. *Titus Groan.* London: Eyre & Spottiswoode, 1946.

Shippey, Tom. *J. R. R. Tolkien: Author of the Century*. London: HarperCollins, 2000.

Smith, Sherwood. *Oached Pish*, LiveJournal weblog. http://sartorias.livejournal.com

Stoklasa, Mike. Review of *Star Wars: Revenge of the Sith* at Red Letter Media. Online at http://redlettermedia.com/plinkett/star-wars/star-wars-episode-iii-revenge-of-the-sith/

Swift, Jonathan. *Gulliver's Travels: an annotated text with critical essays*. New York: W. W. Norton, 1961.

Tolkien, J. R. R. *The Fellowship of the Ring*. 2nd ed. London: Allen & Unwin, 1966.

—*The Letters of J. R. R. Tolkien*. London: Allen & Unwin, 1981.

—*The Return of the King*. 2nd ed. London: Allen & Unwin, 1966.

—*Tree and Leaf*. 3rd ed. London: HarperCollins, 2001.

—*The Two Towers*. 2nd ed. London: Allen & Unwin, 1966.

Willey, Basil. 'The limitations of satire'. Critical essay in Swift, *Gulliver's Travels*, edition cited above.

Wodehouse, P. G. *Very Good, Jeeves*. London: Herbert Jenkins, 1930.

Wolverton, Dave. 'On Writing as a Fantasist'. Online at http://www.sff.net/people/dtruesdale/wolverton1.htp

Specific references by chapter

Death carries a camcorder

'I have a strong dislike': Sherwood Smith, *Oached Pish*. Online at http://sartorias.livejournal.com/154279.html

'Looking at the little abortive Secondary World': Tolkien, *Tree and Leaf*, 'On Fairy-Stories'.

'In *Beowulf*, I am reliably informed': The quotation and interpretation are from Shippey, *Tolkien*, Afterword (section 'Tolkien and modernism').

'Those who pass the gates of Barad-dûr': Tolkien, *Fellowship*, book II, chapter 4.

'A fox passing through the wood': ibid. book I, chapter 3.

Zeno's mountains

'The Hobbit sequel': Tolkien, *Letters*, no. 31.

'It is now approaching completion': *ibid.* no. 47.

Quakers in Spain

'Food hath been prepared': Eddings, *Castle of Wizardry*, chapter 25.

'You can't clip Pegasus' wings': Le Guin, *Language of the Night*, 'From Elfland to Poughkeepsie'.

'Real archaic English is far more *terse*': Tolkien, *Letters*, no. 171.

Gwladys and the Ghraem'lan

'You sit there and tell me': Wodehouse, *Very Good, Jeeves*, 'The Spot of Art'.

Tyrion 13:4

' "This, sir," replied Silas': Dickens, *Our Mutual Friend*, chapter 6.

Teaching Pegasus to crawl

'When Mr. Bilbo Baggins': Tolkien, *Fellowship*, book I, chapter 1.

'The sun was already sinking': Brooks, *Sword of Shannara*, chapter 1.

'The dark figure was almost on top': *ibid.*

'On the morning of his leaving': Hancock, *Greyfax Grimwald*.

'She came out of the store just in time': Donaldson, *Lord Foul's Bane*.

'The Wheel of Time turns': Jordan, *The Eye of the World*, chapter 1.

All hats are grey in the dark

'A mass of truly horrible characters': Glenda Larke, 'Ten things I hate to see in a book meme'.

'When a man is getting better': Lewis, *Mere Christianity*, book III, chapter 4.

Sock Puppet, son of Sock Puppet

'Poly phrase: The idea of line marriage': Mistress Matisse.

Campbell's Cream of Fantasy

'The general assumption': Le Guin, *Language*, 'From Elfland to Poughkeepsie'.

'When you hear a new violinist': *ibid.*

'The books I write are first of all novels': Goodkind, talk at Borders.

The Leaden Rule

'It might be stated this way': Chesterton, *Orthodoxy*, chapter 4.

'If you draw a giraffe': *ibid.* chapter 3.

'They think that [God] works like the factories': Lewis, *Pilgrim's Regress*, book 8, chapter 9.

'Oft evil will shall evil mar': Tolkien, *The Two Towers*, book III, chapter 11.

'Oft the unbidden guest': *ibid.* chapter 7.

'It needs but one foe to breed a war': Tolkien, *The Return of the King*, book VI, chapter 5.

'See the bear in his own den': Lewis, *The Horse and His Boy*, chapter 4.

'He who waits for the sword': Donaldson, *Lord Foul's Bane*, chapter 15.

'Perfect speed is being there': Bach, *Jonathan Livingston Seagull*.

'People are stupid': Goodkind, *Wizard's First Rule*, chapter 36.

'The Wizard's Fourth Rule': Goodkind, *Temple of the Winds*, chapter 41.

'Life is the future': Goodkind, *The Pillars of Creation*, chapter 60.

'Deserve Victory': Goodkind, *Naked Empire*, chapter 61.

'I was angry with my friend': Blake, 'A Poison Tree'.

'If there's more than one way to do a job': Attributed to Edward A. Murphy, Jr., by his son Robert, in *People*, January 31, 1983, p. 82.

Why are dragons afraid of Americans?

'end up watching bloody detective thrillers': Le Guin, *Language*, 'Why Are Americans Afraid of Dragons?'

'Examination of a large number of these papers': Orwell, 'Boys' Weeklies'.

'Lacking training and encouragement': Le Guin, *op. cit.*

'He claimed that authors had gone astray': Wolverton, 'On Writing as a Fantasist'.

'The Ford car has done an awful lot of harm': Lynd & Lynd, *Middletown*, p. 254.

'What do you say to a docker': *New Statesman*, vol. 114, p. 11.

Creative discomfort and *Star Wars*

'The fact is that this script feels rushed': Stoklasa, review of *Revenge of the Sith,*
    part 3.

'They're already building sets': George Lucas, quoted in Stoklasa, *loc. cit.*

'Before you take a decision': Cleese, SMI talk on creativity.

'This is the story of Mace Windy': George Lucas, quoted in Kaminski, *Secret
    History.*

'[Lucas] contacted the elderly Brackett': Kaminski, *op. cit.*

' "I'll bet you a box of bonbons against—" ': Mitchell, *Gone With the Wind,* chap-
    ter 17.

'Afraid I was gonna leave': Kershner, *The Empire Strikes Back.*

Ad effigiem

'What I thought altogether unaccountable': Swift, *Gulliver's Travels,* book III,
    chapter 2.

'Thinning': article of that title in Clute & Grant, *Encyclopedia of Fantasy.*

'the difficult feat of making out modern life': Orwell, *Inside the Whale,* title es-
    say.

'When they began to talk': Swift, *Gulliver,* book IV, chapter 11.

'His Name was *Pedro de Mendez*': *ibid.*

'Bentham, says Mill, habitually missed': Basil Willey, 'The limitations of satire', in
    Swift, *Gulliver's Travels* (Norton edition).

ABOUT THE AUTHOR

Tom Simon is a lifelong reader of fantasy, science fiction, and other works of the imagination. He first discovered this vice before his fourth birthday, when his father taught him to read with a shelf of Dr. Seuss books and a tape recorder. A year or so later, he discovered the Oz books and *Winnie-the-Pooh,* and has never looked back, except to wonder exactly where he is and how he got there.

Early in life he began to notice that some books worked well and left a lasting impression, and others didn't. He began inquiring into the causes, opening up stories and taking them apart to see what made them tick, playing the game that Kipling calls 'Why What Did That'. This introduced him to his second vice – Criticism – which he has been indulging, off and on, ever since, for the amusement of a small but loyal readership.

From time to time, at deadly risk of being considered a hypocrite, he tries to apply his critical lessons to the writing of actual stories. His first fantasy novel, *Lord Talon's Revenge,* was published in 2012. He is also making his own journey through 'Zeno's mountains' with a series called *The Eye of the Maker,* which he thinks a lot more people should buy.

Tom Simon lives in the Frozen North with no company but a polar bear, two musk oxen, and an occasional visit from a travelling ptarmigan. His igloo, however, is centrally heated by a smelly campfire, which also provides him with a connection to the outside world via high-speed smoke signals. He is widely known for his utter and inflexible devotion to telling the truth, except when writing about himself in the third person.

14404938R00092

Printed in Germany
by Amazon Distribution
GmbH, Leipzig